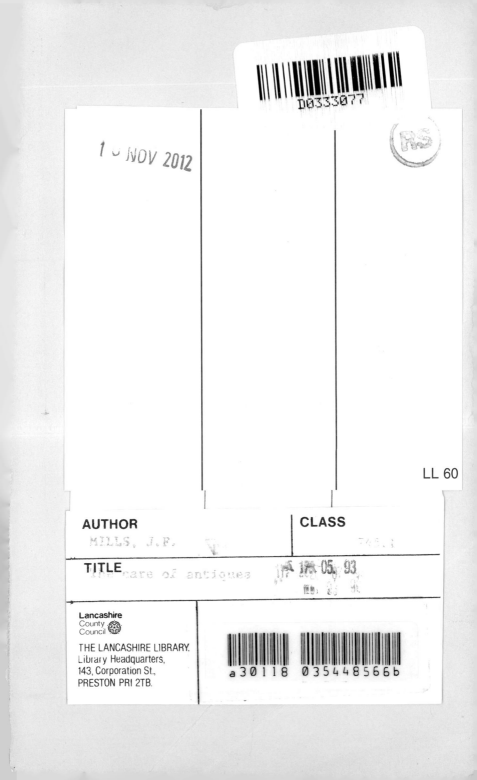

The Care of
ANTIQUES

The Care of
ANTIQUES

JOHN FITZMAURICE MILLS

Preface by A. E. Werner,
formerly Keeper of the Research Laboratory,
British Museum, London.

Foreword by Norman Brommelle,
formerly Keeper of the Conservation Department,
Victoria and Albert Museum, London.

ARLINGTON BOOKS  London

THE CARE OF ANTIQUES
First published 1964 by
Arlington Books (Publishers) Ltd
15–17 King St, St James's
London SW1

Reprinted 1965, 1966, 1968, 1969
First published in a revised paperback edition 1980
Reissued 1988

© *John Fitzmaurice Mills 1964, 1980*

Printed and bound in Great Britain by
Billing & Sons Ltd, Worcester

ISBN 0 85140 518 5

CONTENTS

Preface

A NUMBER OF BOOKS HAVE APPEARED FROM TIME TO TIME dealing with the restoration of antiques, and therefore it is natural to enquire what is the special feature which may serve to distinguish this present book from those that have preceded it. I feel that the answer lies in the fact that the author has taken particular care to present the technical aspects of the subject not only in a logical manner but also in a refreshingly individualistic style so that this book cannot be regarded as merely following the common pattern; one is always conscious of the author's personal delight in the inherent beauty of the objects themselves, and his desire that they should receive the care they deserve so they may be preserved from the ravages of time and the consequences of neglect.

In describing the methods and materials that are now available for the preservation and restoration of antiques the author has been careful to distinguish between the kind of work which can with confidence be undertaken by the intelligent amateur and that which requires special skill and should best be left to the professional restorer. I feel confident, indeed, that the author has succeeded in realising the principal purpose of this work, namely to provide the owner of antiques (or any person responsible for their care) with a framework within which he can safely proceed to build up his knowledge of the modern practice of restoration and deepen his appreciation of the care which should be devoted to preserving antiques and works of art—those silent witnesses of the skill and creative ability of the craftsmen of the past.

A. E. WERNER

Foreword

EVERY HOUSEHOLD HAS AT LEAST A FEW OBJECTS, SUCH as china, furniture, and paintings which the owner regards with pride as having some value, aesthetic or sentimental. These get broken, damaged and ill treated in an extraordinary variety of ways. Children shoot arrows at them, cleaners drop them, they are scorched in fires and fall from the wall at the exact moment of Aunt Jane's death. The valuable Sheraton cabinet which mysteriously cracks during the cold spring of 1962, cracks again, in more places, during the cold winter of 1963. The family portraits become progressively yellower and more obscure.

The sensible owner will find a competent professional restorer. The restorer will know how to clean and repair the object so that in the end it will be as near as possible to the artist's original intention, bearing in mind, however, the fact that the true patina of age (which must not be confused with dirt) should be preserved. The less sensible owner will get to work himself with soap and water, methylated spirits and do-it-yourself glues. Sometimes the result will be satisfactory, but there is a chance that it will be disastrous. Irreparable damage can be done in a few seconds by the most simple and apparently harmless materials. The professional not only knows what to do, and how to do it, but he also knows, usually by bitter experience, when to leave things alone.

There still remains, however, a limited field in which the unskilled owner can operate with comparative safety, provided that he learns a little about the basic properties of the materials, wood, metal, stone, paint and so on of which art objects are composed. If he does so, he will not be able to carry out the major operations, but at least he will be able to do a little minor surgery, and, more important, avoid the conditions under which deterioration is accelerated. Most artifacts are likely to be damaged by particular treatments or particular environmental factors, and it is common sense to know what these sensitive factors are, and avoid them if possible. Thus water colours, miniatures and dye-stuffs of textiles are likely to be faded in strong light, especially daylight, whereas furniture is not much affected by light but will warp and crack in the dry air of overheated rooms in winter. Some materials are affected by the sulphurous atmosphere of cities, and others by the salt-laden atmosphere of coastal districts. John Mills devotes a considerable amount of space in this book to describing the effects of adverse environmental factors and how these effects can be minimised and the objects protected against them. This is conservation, the 'preventive medicine' of the subject, which, if properly understood and applied can make most restoration unnecessary. The simpler cleaning and restoration treatments which Mr. Mills also describes in detail can be carried out by the owner if he is careful and cautious. The more advanced treatments, some of which are also described, are best left alone, though it is valuable to understand the scope of what is professionally possible.

There is one drawback in a handbook of this kind, however practical and comprehensive. Every object has its own particular characteristics so that a treatment, recommended as generally applicable to a type of object may have to be judiciously modified to obtain the best results. Consequently the specialist when consulted by telephone, often cautiously remarks that he would have to see the object before making any recommendations. Careful readers of this handbook will however usually be able to judge which treatment is applicable to a particular case, and, if there is any doubt at all should consult a specialist.

NORMAN BROMMELLE

Acknowledgments

THE AUTHOR WISHES TO EXPRESS HIS GRATITUDE TO THE many people and firms who have assisted in the preparation of this book, in particular: Dr. A. E. Werner, Norman Brommelle, A. D. Baynes-Cope, H. Barker, Miss Mavis Bimson, D. F. Bisset, E. R. Beecher, and Karen Finch. For information regarding the American materials the author is indebted to Caroline Keck of Cooperstown, New York, and Clement Silverstro of the American Association for State & Local History.

The author is indebted to the Victoria & Albert Museum for permission to publish all the photographs in this book, with the exception of those in Plates 41–44, for which he extends his gratitude to Karen Finch.

1 *Furniture*

THE SOUL OF A GREAT TREE CAN LIVE ON FOR CENTURIES after it has been cut down. Man's use of timber for furniture dates back to some of the earliest Egyptian dynasties and further. Wood is one of the greatest friends he has.

Even to-day, with all the modern synthetic materials, it is still timber in one form or another that is called upon to make our tables, chairs, beds and the rest of our furniture. In the history of furniture making an immense variety of different woods have been called in, either on account of their structural characteristics or because of the beautiful grain and colour which they will exhibit when treated. Exotic timbers such as amaranth, amboyna, mahogany, olive, have been imported from far overseas; local woods such as laburnum, walnut and various fruit-woods have been used as inlay or veneer to add their qualities to the strength and charm of oak, beech, elm and pine.

Timber, even when hundreds of years old, can still have strange and unpredictable characteristics: the old, iron-hard oak chest, made in the 17th century or earlier, can move and warp with changes of relative humidity as though it were only a few years old.[1]

The various woods that have been used in fine furniture making have come from widely varying conditions of temperature, humidity, and often two or more types are employed in the same piece. Works of craftsmanship need love and thought, and much can be done to prolong their life by what are quite often simple precautions. Two of the greatest enemies of wood in

[1] See Appendix.

furniture are temperature and humidity. Of these two, it is extremes of humidity that will do the most damage.

One of the comforts of modern living is central heating. This can spell risk for furniture unless some precautions are taken. It is when winter sets in and the central heating plant is really brought into action that trouble begins; outside the temperature can be low, even freezing, but inside, very probably, a comparatively high temperature of between 65° and 70°F. will be maintained by the radiators or air ducts. Both of these at the same time, will tend to make the air dry; thus, if you have a high temperature inside, with a low humidity, a condition is produced which is liable to produce cracking in woodwork. It should be understood that cold air can hold less moisture than hot air. If your house has localized sources of heat such as radiators or fireplaces, then, whenever possible, furniture of value should be kept away from these points. Often, the danger can be alleviated by quite a small lowering of the overall room temperature; sometimes central heating is as high as 75°F., and even by lowering this by 10°F., you automatically raise the degree of relative humidity by approximately 5°, which could bring it into a safe region for your furniture.

Fluctuation of overall heat should also be avoided if possible, because if you have a great rise and fall in the temperature it means that the wood will be in a constant state of 'working'. Draughts, on the same principle, should be avoided, for if they are intermittent it will again mean a rise and fall of temperature. A hard, dry, cold spell in winter can produce the worst conditions of all, as during this time the rate of relative humidity is likely to be very low. Under such conditions one way of raising the relative humidity would be to place shallow trays of water over the radiator or heat sources with pieces of hessian or sacking half sticking out, so that they would form a wick, which could increase the moisture of the air. In certain cases this might be accelerated by having a small electric fan playing over the water tray and wick.

Attack by fungi and insects is second only to damage from humidity and temperature. Generally speaking, in a properly warm house, conditions will not be present which would encourage the growth of fungus. These fungi need a certain degree of dampness and stagnant air in which to flourish. The most likely timber to be affected is that which is actually incorporated into the building, such as beams and carved timber overmantels. These are in contact with stone or brickwork which may be damp owing to the lack of a damp-proof course. The wall may also be damp from being in contact with earth outside the building, as when a house is set into a hill. One of the most deadly fungi is the virulent dry-rot which is extremely difficult to eradicate without large sacrifices of the material affected. Dry-rot can very quickly remove the substance of the timber and reduce it to a dry, powdery state. The fungus can spread rapidly, and immediate treatment should be sought as soon as the condition has been discovered. Specialist knowledge is, however, often required.

If the timbers affected are structural in the building, or built into stone walls preventative measures which can be taken include the installation of a damp-course and treating the wall itself with preparations for the control of rising damp. To remove the stagnant air which carries the spores and encourages the growth of the fungus, proper ventilation should be introduced. The end wood of timbers can be impregnated with some kind of water-proofing agent such as linseed oil or wax. Where carved or valuable timbers are outside, they can be inspected to see if sources of water are dripping on them, and these can be deflected and the base of the timbers impregnated with fungicide. Two of the better of these fungicides for treating timbers and protecting them from the ravages of dry-rot are 'Permosan 116' and 'Cuprinol Penta 116'. These are highly effective chemical compounds, but it is emphasized that the instructions on the containers should be read thoroughly and followed with care. The exact length of protection will vary considerably with both the particular conditions of fungus prevailing, the timber involved, and the previous applications of varnish, stain or wax polish which have been applied to it.

The third enemy of timber, both structural and in fine furniture, is the insect. In many ways, the insect is a greater danger than the first two, as the attack can take place at any time. One of the safeguards is cleanliness. Secretions of dust and dirt in the backs of wood, bad joints in the floor, gaps in the wainscot and floor timbers, are all encouragement to one or other of the insect pests to start his ravaging.

There are four common types of insects which attack woodwork—all wood-borers—and they are: the common furniture beetle, the death-watch beetle, the so called powder-post beetles, and the house longhorn beetle (Fig. No. 1). In all the varieties, it is not the beetle itself that does the damage, but the larvae or grubs. The female beetles normally lay their eggs in cracks in the timber, old joints, and even old woodworm holes from a

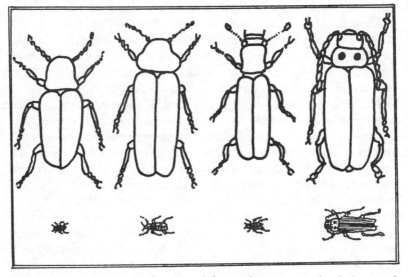

Fig. 1. Wood attacking beetles. From left to right: Furniture beetle (or wood worm), death watch beetle, powder post beetle and house longhorn beetle. The small drawings underneath are life size.

previous infestation. When the eggs hatch, the larvae at once start to burrow through the wood to obtain their food from the timber. In some cases, the larvae state may last for two years or even longer. When full grown, the larvae changes to pupae which remain dormant until changing, after a few weeks, into a fully developed beetle which then gnaws its way out of the timber. It is usually in the spring or early summer that the first signs of infestation appear; these are tiny, light coloured piles of powder on the floor underneath the pieces of wood attacked. After emerging, the beetle then lays its eggs within a few days, and once more the cycle of damage is begun. Furniture and timbers of a house should be inspected regularly each year to detect the attack in its infancy or before it has reached its height.

The characteristics of environment liked by the woodworm, besides dirt and the wood are dampness, from these it can make its base. Three-ply wood, made from cheap deal, is a real banquet for the wood-boring beetle, and this wood should never be allowed in a house at all. The modern, artificially produced hard-boards are greatly superior for backing pictures, screens and other purposes for which three-ply wood has been used.

Treatment for woodworm, in one or other of its manifestations, is a difficult process, and one in which it is hard to assess the degree of success. The problem is to make certain that the insecticide material really reaches the larvae which may often be inches down into the wood. There are two methods: the first, fumigation; and the second, the use of some form of liquid insecticide. Certainly, fumigation is the most effective and reliable method of killing off woodworm completely, although fumigation by itself will not give lasting protection. The application of a liquid, for real protection, should be done hole by hole, to make certain that each larva has been killed.[2] With a badly infested piece of wood, this will need a great deal of patience, and also observation to make sure that none are missed. As to the time of protection from proprietary woodworm killers, this will again vary with the type of timber, atmospheric conditions; but, if properly applied, it should be at the minimum twelve months, and may extend to several years. Once the worm has been killed, it is most important that all possible grounds for egg-laying should be completely eradicated. Scrupulous cleanliness is necessary, and this, with the filling of cracks in the woodwork with a wax, will go a long way towards removing possible breeding grounds. The common furniture beetle is the most prevalent type of insect. It does not favour newly seasoned wood, but likes a timber which is fifteen years or more old, and will work from sap to heart-wood. It particularly likes plywood from alder and birch which is bonded with animal glue. The death-watch beetle drills a much larger hole, and favours old timber, hardwoods such as oak, and is mostly found attacking the large structural timbers such as those found in old country houses, churches and similar buildings. Although it will attack softwood, it is nearly always found in hardwood. The powder-post beetle, too, will not attack soft-wood; it likes the sap-wood of such trees as ash, elm, oak and

[2] See Appendix.

walnut; the preference is for unseasoned or recently seasoned timbers. The longhorn beetle is an extremely destructive pest on the Continent but has also made its appearance in the south-east of England. It likes a new, freshly seasoned softwood, and makes a hole about the same size as the death-watch beetle; it will not attack hardwoods, and infestation in a building usually starts in the roof timbers or attics.

One other form of furniture of vegetable origin which can encourage insect infestation is basketry. Owing to the soft, absorbent nature of the basket-work, liquid insecticide is more effective than with hardwood, as even if it is not actually squirted into the holes, it will soak into the structure of the material and reach the active larvae. But, of course, an insect attack on a soft material like basket-work can be infinitely quicker in its effect than on wood, and a single breeding cycle can ruin a piece.

If a valuable piece of furniture has been particularly badly attacked by woodworm, and the attack has not been noticed owing either to storage or some other reason, modern methods of impregnation can still save the piece and give it further life. Synthetic resins and bonding agents can be soaked into the material to bind the honeycombed wood together and to give it reasonable permanence. This, of course, is a task for an expert, and advice should be taken on it.

The patina of old wood is one of its greatest attractions. To a piece of furniture it gives a subtlety of harmony which no amount of French polish and faking can ever approach. The soft tones of oak, 300 years or more old, which carries the scratches and scars of age with dignity, give an atmosphere which is one of the attractions of real antique furniture. To possess it is a joy, and to look after it is a duty. To-day, there are dozens of different polishes on the market, that range from tins of wax pastes that need a great deal of muscle power, to the aerosol spray with liquid polish that will gleam at a wipe.

A good polish should really do two things: it should remove dirt, and it should give a lasting protection to the surface of the wood. If it is in constant use, one other characteristic should be that it will show finger-marks to the minimum. One of the finest polishes for wood and leather is a wax paste than can be easily and quickly prepared from 3 ounces of purified beeswax, 8 fluid ounces of turpentine and 8 fluid ounces of water. Break up the beeswax into small pieces and melt in a saucepan over low heat. When completely liquid, remove from the heat and pour in the turpentine, followed by the water, and stir rapidly to achieve an even mix. Finally, add a few drops of ammonia to thicken the mixture to a cream. The consistency can be thinned by slightly decreasing or increasing the amounts of turpentine and water. Stir constantly until the polish cools and then store in screw-top jars. This process is not quite so alarming as it sounds, but fire precautions should be taken. This fine polish should be sparingly applied with a soft duster or pad of cotton wool, rubbed in, and then left for about an hour, finally being brought up with a soft duster, a chamois leather or velvet pad. If an electric polisher is available, a fine polish can be obtained but great care should be taken. A good polish is 'Antiquax' available from quality ironmongers. If desired, a homemade beeswax polish can be quite simply made by melting one ounce of beeswax in three fluid ounces of turpentine. For veneer work a furniture cream is more suitable. But whatever type of polish is applied, it is important that it should not be put on too lavishly, as any excess of polish can lead to a smearing of the patina which can be very difficult to eradicate, it may even necessitate a cleansing of the surface with a mild solvent such as turpentine substitute to remove the excess of wax.

During the 19th century, French polish was introduced as a finish for furniture. This polish is produced by treating the surface of the wood with shellac in spirit, the process being to build up layer upon layer of the shellac until the depth and quality of the gloss is achieved. French polish is sometimes treated with fine glasspapers to emulate a wax polish, but it is a process which is not likely to deceive a practised eye. Scratches in French polish can be treated if they are not too deep, by rubbing into them a little hard wax that has been softened by heat. If the scratch is broad, or goes deeper and shows the naked wood underneath, it may be necessary first to apply a little water stain to tone the wood down before rubbing in the wax. The best kind of wax for this purpose is beeswax which has had a little resin melted into it to increase the hardness when cool.

There are many cases of furniture prior to the 19th century

that have been mistakenly treated with French polish and heavy varnishes to 'improve' their appearance. With care, this French polish and varnish can be removed. One or other of the commercial paint strippers are suitable, such as 'Polystrippa' or 'Nitromors', and this should be applied carefully with a small piece of cotton wool. When using a paint stripper of any kind, it is advisable to protect the hands with rubber gloves. The paint stripper should be left on the surface of the wood for a few minutes and then wiped off with clean cotton wool. After that, the whole surface of the treated wood should be well washed down with turpentine substitute to remove any remaining paint stripper, dissolved varnish or polish. If the piece being treated has complicated carving this can best be got at by using an old toothbrush, or, in very delicate cases, a small cheap paintbrush. Once again it should be washed down afterwards very thoroughly with turpentine substitute. If it is a question of working over inlay of any kind, extreme care should be exercised and only a very small piece of the surface should be treated at a time, even using a tiny piece of cotton wool wrapped round a matchstick and dipped into the solvent. After the turpentine substitute has dried off, wax polishing can be resumed in the normal manner. It should be noted that the removal of varnish or French polish from a valuable piece of furniture should be carried out with care as the original maker may have applied a varnish or lacquer coating that would be invisible underneath later laid coats. Therefore, a professional restorer should be consulted whenever there is any doubt.

At sales, particularly in the country, old pieces of furniture may often be purchased which hide their beauty under layers of grime and filth accumulated over the years. One of the most effective ways of clearing this grime is to make a cleaning emulsion, which, incidentally, will polish at the same time. This can be prepared by mixing together one part each of linseed oil, vinegar and turpentine with a quarter of a part of methylated spirit. The mixture should be shaken vigorously each time before use.

One point often overlooked when polishing or cleaning any veneered furniture is that sometimes a corner of the veneer may have lifted. Considerable damage may be caused by the polisher catching in this, and lifting it further. One of the most frequent causes of damage to polish, and the colour of good furniture is exposure to sunlight. It will fade French Polish and often the underlying wood. The sun will cause the polished surface to deteriorate and tend to bleach the colour from the wood, often, in a few weeks, ruining the beautiful patina which may have taken centuries to produce. The remedying of such a condition is a difficult process, and should, for the safety of a good piece, be left to an expert. But experiment can be made if the instructions below are carefully carried out.

First of all, the polishing wax or surface French polish should be removed with turpentine to which a little methylated spirit has been added. The surface of the wood should be allowed to dry out, and then lightly washed with vinegar and water. When this, too, has been allowed to dry off a mixture of equal parts of linseed oil and turpentine should be rubbed into the faded portions only and immediately wiped off before the colour has deepened too much. After this, lightly French polish the treated surface, and put in, with a brush or cotton wool, the tones that have bleached; the medium should be a diluted polish with colours such as burnt umber, raw umber, burnt sienna added to it. Finally, several days later apply once more a little French polish and then finish with your normal furniture polish.

This kind of damage, caused by the sun, can also be evident in the cracking of the wood, particularly with small objects carved images. Again, this has been caused by undue warming-up of the surface layers while the interior wood is still cold. Treatment here is possibly best carried out with a beeswax polish, which will feed, as well as bring back the patina of the wood. A softer version of a beeswax polish can be made by dissolving beeswax in turpentine which has been heated in a double boiler. The right consistency is that of butter once it is cool.

Many types of chairs have basket-work, cane-work or rush-work seats and backs. These materials are best cleaned by a moderate use of a weak solution of soap in warm water. The liquid should be applied with a moist sponge or piece of cotton wool, afterwards dried off thoroughly and left for twenty-four hours. As a protective coat, a thin solution of acrylic resin such as 'Bedacryl 122X' may be applied. This will help to consolidate the basket-work and protect it, preventing grime rubbing into the surface, and will also help to bind any pieces of the basket-work or cane which may be splitting or tending to flake away.[2] Another method to help preserve the life of the material is, after cleaning with 'Lissapol' froth, and thorough drying, to impregnate it with a purified, bleached beeswax that has been dissolved in benzene.

Leather may be used in furniture as the tops of desks and tables, seats and backs of chairs and other forms of upholstery; also as the covering material in screens, sometimes ornamented, stained or just left in its natural condition. Leather is liable to attack from insects, and also, in extremely damp conditions, to fungal growths. Leather becomes prone to fungal attack when the humidity rises, so that in a relative humidity of the atmosphere above 68% mould growths are permitted. These may affect the colour of the leather by staining and may also attack the surface texture, and, with stained leather, the colours may be drastically altered. In the first case, the use of fungicide may arrest, but not necessarily cure, the condition. The steps to take are to ensure adequate ventilation and also to dry out thoroughly the pieces affected. Where it is necessary to apply a fungicide, especially in over-humid conditions found in warm climates, one should be chosen with a negative amount of staining or rotting qualities, and one which is also of a low volatility. A most reliable fungicide for leather is 'Paranitrophenol'. This will cause a slight yellow stain in too strong a concentration but, when employed very diluted in water or alcohol to a strength of 0.35%, its discoloration is minimal. Another is 'Pentachlorophenol' which should also be employed as a very weak solution, 0.25%. During the war, these two fungicides were mixed together in equal parts by weight, and were found to be an extremely effective preservative for leather against fungoid attacks; indeed, they were issued in such form to the U.S. Army when despatched on tropical service. For prolonged periods of protection, it may be necessary to increase the strength of the solution. Owing to the yellow staining propensity of Paranitrophenol it is better to use the second, Pentachlorophenol. The commercial name for the sodium salt is Santobrite, and it may be dissolved either in water or alcohol to a 2% solution. Another fungicide for leather is Mystox L.P.2, a preparation in paraffin solution which may be sprayed on. Leather is liable to attack by several types of insect including

[2] See Appendix.

moth and other parasites. If the article is of extreme value, and the infestation severe, the best course is professional fumigation by hydrogen cyanide or carbon disulphide; both these will kill the insects, but will not give a lasting protection.

One of the best preservatives for leather, whether as a piece of upholstery, a screen, or desk-top or bookbinding, is the British Museum leather dressing. This is prepared by mixing together anhydrous lanolin, 7 ozs. with cedarwood oil, 1 fl. oz. beeswax, ½ oz. and hexane 11 fl. ozs. These can be mixed by dissolving the beeswax in the hexane first, then adding the lanolin and lastly, the cedarwood oil. The hexane is extremely inflammable, and no naked flame or source of open heat should be present while mixing it or whilst it is being used. When made, it is a thin yellow cream, and should be applied sparingly with a piece of cotton wool or soft rag, to the surface of the leather, rubbed well in, and left for two days, when it may then be polished with a soft cloth or brush. The leather dressing is highly penetrative, and will do much to restore the substance and life of the leather, leaving behind a soft sheen and very pleasant cedar smell. Any cleaning, or mending or glueing down of a piece of leather that is lifting from a desk-top, should be done before the application of the dressing, as the oils and waxes will stop glues taking properly. Leather that is extremely grimy, if not in a split and peeling condition, can be safely washed. Before you do this, gently test, with a small moist brush, to make sure the colour will not run. Then wash gently with lukewarm water and a pure soap, using the minimum of moisture to remove the dirt. Pure soap is one without excess alkali or rosin, of similar quality to a high grade toilet soap. Stains on the leather may often be removed with a mild solvent such as white spirit or petrol, applied with small pieces of cotton wool. If the stains are obstinate, it is often better to leave them rather than to rub too hard, or the leather may be spoilt.

In the case of leather coverings that have come away from a desk-top or screen and need fixing, first of all, as much of the old glue as possible should be removed by scraping away with a sharp knife. The type of glue for refixing may be an aqueous one such as rabbit-skin, but if this is applied, the leather should be moistened as little as possible to prevent it buckling. A better type of adhesive is one of the modern synthetic resin emulsion adhesives, preferably internally plasticized especially when permanent flexibility is important.

Where leather work on screens or chair-backs has painted patterns or pictures, these will be brought up as far as possible by the application of British Museum leather dressing, mentioned in a previous paragraph. Gentle attempts to clean the surface further than by soap and water may be made by pure turpentine, but the use of any stronger solvent should be avoided as the paint may be loosened. Colours on leather tend to sink right into the texture of the leather itself and will, almost inevitably, come down in tone. If the leather dressing does not bring the appearance up as much as is thought possible, a further treatment can be to give it a gentle polishing with the furniture cream mentioned earlier in this chapter. Attempts are often made to varnish decorated leather, but this treatment is inadvisable, the principal reason being that the leather, with temperature and humidity, will 'move' considerably, and as it is flexible it may be pushed or temporarily dented in usage when the varnish is liable to crack. Further, the glisten of the varnish is an unnatural appearance with leather, which is at its best with a mellow sheen from polishing.

Tarnished ormolu can often considerably disfigure an otherwise attractive piece of furniture. The cause of tarnishing in ormolu is that the brass underneath sweats through the gold surface finish. The professional would treat this condition with prussic acid, but it is an extremely risky procedure to try in the home. An alternative method, which is reasonably safe, is to use a solution of ammonia, 1 dessertspoonful of 'cloudy' ammonia in a cup of warm water. Although this will not bring the full brightness back to the ormolu, it will considerably improve the appearance. The ammonia should be applied with a swab of cotton wool wrung out before applying, and great care should be taken to see that none of the ammonia gets on to the woodwork. If this solution does not prove strong enough, the strength can be increased. To protect the hands, rubber gloves should be worn.[4] After thorough drying out, polish with the furniture cream, or better still lacquer with 'Ercaline'.

Decorative furniture, frames of mirrors and pictures are often covered with gilded gesso. This can be damaged or rubbed away and all too often layers of later gilding may have been applied.

[4] See Appendix.

Plate 1. *A Boule desk with inlays peeling.*

Plate 2. *Warping of veneer on an early 18th century inlaid walnut cabinet.*

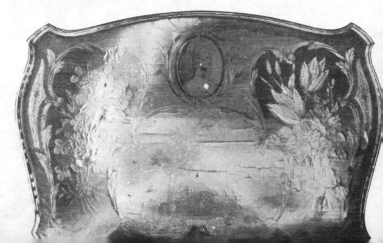

Plate 3. *Ground shrinkage of carcass wood in a small table-top.*

Plate 4. Lifting and fracturing of veneer on a drawer front.

Plate 5. Shrinkage in the wood has caused the veneer to buckle.

Plate 6. Shrinkage of the veneer itself and deterioration of the glue has caused this lifting on the large table-top.

Plate 7. *Damage to the veneer round an 18th century knife case, probable causes change in relative humidity and temperature.*

Plate 8. **Typical** *damage that can happen to a table-top panel that is clamped at both ends.*

9. Close-up detail of age in a clamped l, showing not only ting but fracturing.

late 10. Damage to table-top where the eneer and carcass wood are running in the same direction, but they have been prevented from shrinking by having bearers underneath going in the

Plate 11. The effect of over-humidity, drying and heat on the thick wood of a large cloisonné.

Plate 12. The same piece as Plate 11 after treatment.

Plate 13. *The intermediate stage in the restoration of old handle and screw marks.*

Plate 14. *The intermediate stage in the restoration of a japanned cabinet where the lacquer surface had flaked away owing to shrinkage of the carcass wood.*

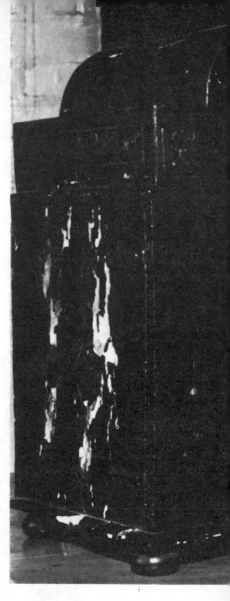

Plate 15. Seventeenth-century cabinet with flaking gesso, paint and varnish.

Plate 16. Typical wearing of upholstery, from friction of legs when in use.

Plate 17. Damage to gilding and gesso caused by movement of the carcass wood.

Plate 18. Another example of damage to gilding and gesso. This can happen in a piece 200 years old even today if it is moved from one atmospheric condition to another.

Plate 19. An 18th century Dummy Board

Plate 20. Preparing a resting bed for the face of a valuable carved panel before it was rebacked.

Plate 21. The resting bed in place.

Plate 22. The carved panel after re-backing with the face undamaged because of careful protection.

These may be layers of bronze powders with size or cellulose lacquers, which tend to obscure the patina, the truth of the original. The removal of layers of later gilding from the original work is difficult without the risk of causing damage and may, in some cases, be impossible. The general principle is to establish a solvent 'differential' between the later and original layers. This will depend upon the nature of the material used. For instance, if the lower layer is water gilding and the upper layer is oil or cellulose lacquer gilding it would be reasonably safe to try toluene, and, if that is too slow, toluene mixed with alcohol or acetone. Mixtures of equal parts of alcohol and benzene might also prove to be effective. Other solvents which might be tried include 'Cellosolve' and Ethylene dichloride. Any attempt at using solvents should, of course, be carried out on a very small area, if possible in a place at the side or back of the piece being treated, so that it will not show if the original gilding material comes away. The best method of application, in the first instance, is with a matchstick with a piece of cotton wool wrapped round it. If the upper layers dissolve, but it is found that the inevitable friction used is affecting the original layers, the procedure should be changed to using a mixture of equal parts of alcohol, 'Cellosolve' and diacetone alcohol. This should not be applied by rubbing but by holding a swab soaked in the mixture in position for a short time. The effect here should be that the mixture will cause the upper layers to swell, and they may then be gently swabbed off with another swab of cotton wool soaked in turpentine. The solvents mentioned here are highly inflammable, and benzene is also poisonous to inhale. Precautions for ventilation and fire should be duly taken.

Closely allied to this gilding problem is the occurrence where silver-leaf has been used, for instance on the carved frame of mirrors. Frequently the silver will have tarnished almost completely black as the result of age and exposure to atmosphere. Aluminium paint is often used in an attempt to bring back the 'effect'. Again, the approach should be extremely cautious, a very small area being tried first. A solvent used in the first instance could be pure acetone, and if this does not work by itself, a mixture of about 2 parts methylated spirit to 1 part ammonia could be employed. If this too fails, recourse could be made to a commercial paint stripper such as 'Nitromors' or 'Polystrippa', both these being used in a controlled manner, with great caution. The swabs of cotton wool should be squeezed out before application and the surface well rinsed with turpentine or turpentine substitute after removal.

By knocking, accidental damage, time, the effects of damp or extreme dryness and heat, inlay work of the Boule type may sometimes tend to have the inlay lifted. The replacement of this is possible if care is used. First, the old remaining glue should be scrubbed off the reverse surface of the inlay, and, where possible, scraped from the bed on the surface of the wood. If the reverse of the tortoise-shell or other material is over-smooth, it should be given a gentle 'tooth' with a piece of medium sandpaper and then the adhesive should be applied both to the inlay and to the bed. The choice can rest between an animal glue such as Scotch or rabbits-skin, or one of the more recent range of synthetics such as 'Croid Polystik'. Any replacement of lost portions of the inlay which may be of tortoise-shell, brass, ebony, ivory or silver should be left to an expert. This same comment applies also to marquetry or parquetry, as the selection of the wood, their condition and use, are matters for considerable skill and knowledge.

The habit, such as is employed in Boule work, of covering wood with a combination of metal, tortoise-shell, mother of pearl, bone or ivory, is, basically, a bad form of design, in so far as wood, metal and other substances are not naturally suited to being stuck one to the other. The ordinary animal and fish glues used in the 18th century were not really suitable; modern adhesives can give more satisfactory results although care must be taken to remove excess at once. In Plate No. 1 is an illustration of a piece of Boule in a bad state, which will certainly cause a great deal of trouble, even to an experienced furniture restorer. In this case the brass inlay of the Boule has sprung away from the carcass due to the movement of the wood, and on the top, a band has come right out no doubt accidentally bent and distorted. The problem is to replace the inlay, flatten it and restore the brass, to remove distortion, and then to get it firmly into place again, a task which is difficult even with the most modern adhesives. It is so easy for tiny points of inlay to stick up. These if caught when the piece is being polished, can be ripped right out.

The problem of marquetry and inlay of one wood on another, is of the reaction of the different woods to different atmospheric and heat conditions.[5] In Plate No. 2 can be seen the pediment of an early 18th century inlaid walnut cabinet. Here the ground wood, the carcass wood on which the surface veneer is laid, has warped and twisted. The left-hand part of the pediment shows the corrugations and ridges running right across the grain of the veneer, caused by this warping of the ground which forms the backing of the veneer. Plate No. 3 shows an example of a shrinkage of the carcass wood which takes place in the normal way. This little table-top has no clamps at the end; therefore, the whole of the top can shrink quite freely; it has shrunk far more than the thin coating of veneer woods which decorate the top, these have been forced into ridges to accommodate the layers to the smaller area to which the carcass has shrunk. A similar phenomenon can be seen in plate no. 4. Here the veneer has been laid on the drawer front at right angles to the direction of the grain of the ground wood. The wood, of course, always shrinks more in its width, and by so doing, does not allow space enough for the superimposed veneer to lie flat. Thus it can start up at the corners, or even, in places, actually be fractured. Plate No. 5 shows this more clearly. Here a band of veneer is running right across the grain of the carcass wood. The wood itself has shrunk and the veneer, being in the opposite direction, has not shrunk and so has not enough space to lie flat. The result is that it will buckle, as seen in the illustration. Treatment will need the care of a professional.

Sometimes veneer is laid in very large pieces, as can be seen in Plate No. 6 on this round table-top, the whole of which has been produced from 4 large sections of veneer bisected by a cross pattern. In this example the veneer itself has shrunk. Owing to a certain amount of deterioration in the animal glue that has been used to hold it down, it has started to peel at the corners and exterior edges. This is a further example of the strain which can be set up when 2 pieces of wood are fastened together with their respective grains running at right angles to the other.

Movement of antique furniture from one locality to another, from one house to another, is always a matter of risk—risk from a change in humidity, change in warmth, different methods of heating. Damage may result up to several months after the change, particularly with veneered furniture. In Plate No. 7 can be seen

[5] See Appendix.

an 18th century knife case, where the underwood has tended to move and has forced up the band of marquetry which decorates it.

One of the damages which can occur to a clamped panel, that may be a table or desk-top, is the type of shrinkage and splitting shown in Plate No. 8. This shows a panel that has been veneered with a symmetrical pattern, and it can be seen that the splits across the top are worst in the middle, but disappear when they get to the end, where the panel is held firm by the clamp and prevented from moving. In Plate No. 9 the damage that can occur in a clamped panel can be seen more closely, as can the tearing apart action of the main panel as it attempts to shrink even though it is held firmly at the ends by the clamps. Not only has the wood split, but in places the grain itself has been torn in a lateral direction. It illustrates clearly that one just cannot prevent the wood from contracting when the moisture content falls.

Another form of damage can be seen in Plate No. 10. This is an example of a circular table-top in which both the veneer and the underlying carcass wood are running in the same direction, but it has bearers underneath the table-top which have been placed in an attempt to keep it straight and flat. These bearers have restricted the natural shrinkage of the wood, and so it has split in three directions where there were joins in the underneath ground-wood. Also seen in this plate are the natural scratches and dents from use and age. As recommended earlier in the chapter, regular treatment with a good wax polish, and, for the worst of the scratches, possibly a little coloured powder might be added to the polish so that it would gradually build into the scratch and, to a certain extent, fill it. This could greatly improve the appearance of the surface, although it would take a good deal of time. Generally speaking, it is a bad thing to worry too much about the small scratches and abrasions over the general surface of a piece of furniture, because they represent, as was said earlier, the patina of age. You are destroying the 'feel', the genuine look of age, if they are covered or treated by French polish, varnish, stains, or over-enthusiastic removal or filling methods. In the 19th century there was a tremendous fashion for going over these beautiful old pieces of furniture to rid them of what the Victorians thought of as unsightly marks and blemishes. They felt that perfect mirror finish was to be desired. To-day we deplore such treatment.

The damage of dampness, drying, heat and movement can affect not only thin veneers, but also pieces of considerable thickness. In Plate No. 11 a large chest is shown in which the carcass wood has been built in the normal way that a box or chest would be constructed, namely, with the grain running horizontally. Over this has been laid a fairly thick layer of mahogany in which the grain is running in a perpendicular direction, and this overlay has shrunk and splitting from top to bottom, torn apart, because the wood upon which it is laid cannot shrink in that same direction. The top of the piece shows similar small cracks in the veneer, where the shrinking in the ground-wood has forced the overlay to break open. In Plate No. 12 can be seen the same piece after treatment, showing that in the hands of a skilled restorer much can be done to eradicate and repair damage of this type.

During its life, old furniture is unfortunately often subjected to many indignities, not only in the way of surface treatment with French polish, but also, in the case of articles like desks, sideboards, chests-of-drawers, by the placing of a great variety of handles and fastenings. In Plate No. 13 can be seen an intermediate stage in the restoration of a piece of furniture which, after the original construction had been fitted with an anachronistic handle which had to be removed. After the removal of the handles, naturally, holes and abrasions are left, which have to be filled in by the restorer. This particularly calls for great skill in the placing of the inlays. The inserts then would be finally smoothed and polished to imitate the original surface. Sometimes, if the objects have been treated badly, polished roughly, or a polish treatment including a slight solvent has been used, the marks may reappear. Not only is veneer surface treatment of wood liable to this eruption and damage, but also lacquering or japanning. In Plate No. 14 can be seen a japanned cabinet, where the lacquer surface has flaked away owing to the movement of the carcass wood. The design itself is in relief, and is obtained by applying a coating of gesso, built up in layers in the form of the pattern—in this case, birds and trees and foliage, and the illustration shows the restoration of this bureau in the intermediate stage. The areas that appear white and plain are, in fact, layers of fresh gesso which have been applied to build it up to the level of the original design which stands out in relief. This will, of course, be succeeded by modelling on the surface such pieces as the feathers and wings of the birds consonant with the original modelling. Then, it will finally be lacquered, coloured and gilded to complete the restoration.

Plate No. 15 shows part of a small 17th century cabinet in which the wood has been covered with gesso and painted to imitate a lacquered surface. Movement of the carcass wood has again caused the gesso and painted surface to flake away, and restoration will call for the replacing of the gesso, and then painting and touching in to complete the design.

Upholstery is very seldom the original, particularly if the article, such as a dining-room chair is in constant use. The friction from handling, particularly on the front and side edges of the seat, is very heavy, and the damage appears usually in the form as seen in Plate No. 16 where the material has frayed and torn away, showing the undercovering of the upholstery itself. The question that has to be decided is whether the value of the original or near original fabric covering is sufficient to merit it staying in its frayed and damaged state, or whether it should be replaced with as near as possible contemporary material. Upholstery can be attempted, but, once again, it is a task best left to the professional, not only to produce a workmanlike finish, |but also to prevent damage to the wood of the original chair which carries it.

The movement of carcass wood can cause damage to any surface layer lacking elasticity, in particular, gilded gesso. In Plate No. 17 the gesso, which is laid on the wood to provide a ground for the gilding, has cracked and forced itself up. Little can be done to allay this damage, as the root cause is the wood underneath which cannot be reached. This is damage which can still occur, even in pieces which may be 200 years old, if movement from one atmospheric condition to another takes place. Plate No. 18 shows similar damage to the top of the legs of a side table. In some places the gesso has adhered to it strongly, but the strain imposed upon it by the shrinking of the core wood has ruptured it into a series of vertical and horizontal directions. If the pieces are loose, they can be fixed with one of the modern synthetic glues, or better still with parchment size. Adhesion can be achieved with the others, that have opened to a certain degree, by gently using a brush or thin spatula to insert a layer of glue into the cracks.

Another example of damage by shrinkage is shown in Plate No. 19. This is called a dummy-board, a popular fashion in the

18th century. These dummy-boards were made of planks cross-battened at the back usually with a bracket to enable them to stand upright in a disused fireplace or corner of the room: they were normally covered with a ground of white lead or gesso, and on to this was painted a figure, which might be a domestic with a broom as in this example. Clamps across the back of the figure prevented it from shrinking freely, and, therefore, the example illustrated has split at each join. Treatment can be carried out as follows: taking the battens off the back and closing the boards together can be attempted, but usually this may be fraught with a certain amount of difficulty as the clamps may be very firmly fixed and the nails may come through the front and be bent over under the gesso or ground. It is better if they can be removed. The piece can then be put on to a new backing such as balsa wood, and fastened with a wax resin mixture so that any further movement is eliminated. In this case the gesso ground must be restored and the paintwork touched in.

The conservation, cleaning or mending of an antique is a complex problem. The amount of care necessary throughout the whole process cannot be emphasized too strongly. These antiques are legacies, from 100 years and more ago; they are ours only for our lifetime, and the approach should be with the greatest integrity, and care. In Plates Nos. 20, 21, 22 are illustrations of part of the work which was carried out on a carved wooden panel where the backing-board was warped and cracked. It was necessary to take the backing-board away and substitute another and more permanent support. To do this, the carving had to be laid on its front, which necessitated protection of the contours of the carving from the pressures which would have to be applied during the rebuilding of the panel from the back. In the illustrations it can be seen how a special bed was prepared for the panel; a series of laths were contoured to fit the panel itself, and then covered with layers of foam-rubber to protect the carving during the placing of the new backing board. This protection of the surface of a piece during manipulation is often overlooked, or the pressures underestimated that may be used during the repair. At all times, adequate protection should be provided on the surface of the worker's bench.

One last point: hinges and locks in old furniture, whether of brass, iron or steel, often become corroded and rusted. They may be treated with a normal penetrating oil, which you can get from your garage, or with one or other of the rust-inhibitors such as the proprietary Plus-Gas. After these have been used they should be washed away with turpentine substitute and then a good clean lubricant put on with a good brush, care being taken that none of the inhibitor, the turpentine substitute or the oil gets on to the surrounding woodwork as it may stain or crack and weaken animal glues which have been used in its construction. If a hinge is broken or has to be replaced, and the screws fixing it are obstinate, there is one way which loosens them. This is first to place a little lubricating oil around the head of the screw and then to touch the head of the screw for a second or two with the tip of a red-hot poker. This application of heat can cause expansion and contraction to loosen the screw, and the oil will penetrate and assist the withdrawal.

If any of the metal fittings on furniture are very badly damaged, they may have to be replaced. The important thing is to search out from a supplier the exact copy of the style of the one being replaced. This may sound a tall order but good stores will often carry a large range of brass and steel fittings. These can be given a little feel of age by careful abrasion with a fine sandpaper and an application of dilute nitric acid. Sometimes the fittings can be bought already so well 'aged' that they can pass muster under an expert's eye.

2 *Metals*

THE PRESERVATION OF METALS IN AN ANTIQUE COLLECTION can pose many problems. The variety of metals can include iron, silver, copper and such alloys as steel, bronze and pewter. Some of these will tarnish, others will rust; some are hard and some are soft; others are liable to a 'disease'; nearly all of them require different cleaning techniques. In the past, like other works of art, many have been subjected to gross cleaning methods which may have scratched and bruised them, and, in the worst cases may have scoured and dissolved part of their surface away.

One of the oldest precious metals is silver, and traces of its use can be found as far back as Ur of the Chaldees, and in ancient Egypt. It is a guide to its value in those far off days that when the robbers broke into the tombs it was often the silver they went for before the gold. Silver, since then, has been used for a wide variety of purposes, from domestic utensils to ornaments, often with other metals worked with it, precious stones, and in processes such as niello.

The silversmiths of England have produced in the past centuries some of the most beautiful examples of tableware, candlesticks, vases and bowls. Fortunately, much of this exquisite craftsmanship still survives, having almost miraculously escaped from pillage, fire, battering and misuse for centuries.

The principal malady that affects silver, is tarnish. This is the formation of a thin film of silver sulphide on the surface, and that is the reason why silver in every day use needs fairly regular polishing and cleaning. Tarnish is formed by the exposure to atmosphere; that of cities, carrying far more impurities, will affect it the worst. The sulphur is present in the air in the form of sulphuretted hydrogen that comes from domestic fires, or from nearby industrial fumes from factories. The action is worse in humid, damp weather, and is worst of all during fog and mists when the fumes are held imprisoned low down.

One other source, sometimes unsuspected, can be cheap household paints, which may contain sulphur impurities that are volatile. This may also apply to certain types of paints such as those which contain casein as binding medium that is liable to release volatile sulphur fumes through bacterial action. For a room that houses precious silver, the decorator should be instructed to use either cellulose colours or the old-fashioned good quality oil-paints, based preferably on a titanium white. An even more 'secret agent' against the polish of silver can be textiles that have had a 'finish' treatment applied to them with chemicals that have contained sulphur.

For hundreds of years silver and more recently Sheffield Plate and other silver-plated pieces have, for their regular cleaning, been rubbed with one or other of the many different varieties of cleaning powders. These can range from jeweller's rouge to plate powders, putty powder, crocus powder, Tripoli powder, or even fine emery powders, either rubbed on dry or as a paste mixed with water or methylated spirit. All of these are abrasives, even if their action is almost infinitesmal and their method of cleaning must, inevitably, in the course of time, remove a quantity of the silver as they take away the tarnish deposit. A piece of old silver has only to be inspected to see how the fine chasing or Coat-of-Arms is rubbed down by this treatment. Gradually, the fine intricate work will dull and disappear, fine edges and scrollwork must lose their bravura.

How then can silver best be cleaned to achieve the beautiful bluey-tinted glistening high polish and, at the same time preserve and not damage the pieces? Liquid treatment is certainly the safest, quickest and cheapest, and least likely to damage the piece. For silver that is badly tarnished, the following treatment is recommended. Put a piece of aluminium sheet about 6″ square or a couple of square feet of aluminium foil such as that used for wrapping meat when baking in the oven at the bottom of a large bowl. Place the pieces of silver to be cleaned onto this aluminium, making sure that they all touch it. Next, cover the silver with a hot solution of washing soda in water about 5% strength is sufficient. Do not be alarmed by the effervescence and fumes that rise, the silver is being cleaned by an electro-chemical treatment, and, from time to time pieces can be lifted from the liquid to see how they are progressing. This should of course, be done with rubber gloves on or a pair of wooden tongs with rubber tips, such as would be used for lifting the clothes into and out of an old-fashioned clothes boiler. After the tarnish has disappeared, the pieces of silver should be washed thoroughly in plenty of warm water, and then, if necessary, given a final light polish with a special silver cloth or large pads of cotton wool. Incidentally, when you put silver into the sink to rinse it off, be careful to lay some sort of soft bedding at the bottom of the sink for the pieces to rest on—one or other of the various types of synthetic cleaning cloths, or better still, a couple of square feet of $\frac{3}{4}''$ foam-rubber.

Silver is particularly prone to damage by scratch. In cleaning, it is therefore very important to make sure that the materials used are completely free from any abrasive material. Even a hard piece of skin on a finger can damage the patina and any form of cleaning with a stiff bristled brush on smooth silver should certainly be avoided. A brush is permissible if there is some heavy chasing or modelling. If there are still some obstinate pieces of tarnish or dirt left after the dip, these can be lightly brushed with a little French chalk moistened to a paste either with methylated spirit, or water with 1 or 2 drops of ammonia.

On the market there is an excellent liquid dip which comes in wide-mouthed jars, particularly suitable for cleaning spoons and forks. This goes under the name of 'Silver Dip', and is quite safe for use. The action of it is remarkably quick, and the silver should not be left in longer than the time stated on the label, which is literally a matter of one or two seconds. The tarnish will vanish almost magically as soon as it is placed into the liquid. The rinsing can be equally speedy, a few seconds in warm water. It can then be finished as in the first method, by polishing with a soft cloth, which may be specially impregnated for this purpose. There is no need to use any kind of detergent for washing after the dip or after the washing soda method.

For very large articles that cannot be dipped, the liquid can be applied with a small swab of cotton wool, one area being treated and then rinsed before moving on to the next. The 'Silver Dip' can be used equally well on silver, silver-plate or Sheffield plate. With a worn plate or Sheffield plate, if the base metal is exposed, the time of immersion in the liquid should be very short indeed, almost an instantaneous in and out and the silverware polished immediately after rinsing. The 'Silver Dip' is not inflammable, and is probably best used wearing rubber gloves if the skin is sensitive. One point: if you wish to use this 'dip' for other metals, such as copper or gold, separate jars should be kept and employed for each metal. The reason for this is that if, for example, a gold piece is cleaned in a 'dip' that has previously been used for a number of silver pieces, that have had their tarnish of silver sulphide removed, this may cause a film of silver to be laid on the gold.

To-day there are various lacquers that can be applied to silver which is for exhibition rather than everyday use; articles such as candlesticks, vases, bowls and salvers. One of the better varieties of these lacquers is 'Frigilene'. This can be applied at home with a brush, the piece of silverware first having been completely cleaned and, even more important, de-greased. If there are any traces of grease at all, the lacquer will not adhere properly. This de-greasing can best be done with methylated spirit, a swab of cotton wool and holding the piece in your hand covered with a rubber glove. In a few moments the methylated spirit will evaporate, and the lacquer can be applied with a soft brush, care being taken that the whole of the piece is covered. This will need careful watching if it is an elaborate pattern, and also, as far as possible the layer of lacquer should be of equal thickness. To ensure the piece is completely covered, hold it between yourself and a source of light, so that you can see how far you have gone more easily. A lacquer such as this should give protection for 12 months or longer, although the exact time will be governed to a large extent by the atmosphere, with its impurities, heat and moisture. When the lacquer is starting to perish a streaky effect can be noticed. The old lacquer can then be removed with a solvent such as acetone and another application be made.

Recently, another protective film has been introduced, which is known as 'Silver Shield'. This is a silicone, and the protective film it gives will last a great deal longer: 5, 6 or more years can be expected. The silicone film is thinner than the lacquer, and it is almost impossible to perceive on the polished silver. It is equally suitable for modern or antique silver. It is completely tarnish-resisting, and even after several years, the protective film does not discolour. This method is not suitable for home application, as it has to be applied by means of special spraying equipment, and the firm who carry this out is mentioned at the back of this book.

As well as the atmosphere, one of the great enemies of silver, whether domestic or showpieces, is moisture. In this country it is almost impossible to have pure water supplied, and all the public water has a small degree of protective chlorine in it which can discolour the silver; therefore, after rinsing, it is very important that it is meticulously dried. Moisture in the atmosphere, also, of course, can carry impurities and this will affect silver. When storing silver, it is of first importance that it is done in as 'moisture-proof' a manner as possible. It may be put away wrapped in several layers of soft tissue paper, but again, this tissue paper should be absolutely dry. It might be a wise plan to leave it for half an hour in a very low oven before use, or overnight in an efficient airing cupboard. The same applies to cotton wool, lint or baize or any material that is used to wrap the silver that is to be put away in a drawer or chest. For extra protection over a long period, the wrapped silver can be put into a polythene or plastic bag which it is possible to seal in an airtight manner. There are also special papers and cloths on the market, for wrapping silver, that have been treated with an anti-tarnish compound.

Needless to say, any form of physical restoration or mending of silver should be left to a trained silversmith. In Plate No. 23 can be seen a badly damaged 18th century English silver censer. It can be seen that the rim at the bottom had been severely dented and in parts ripped away. The treatment for this was to dismantle the rim very carefully, retaining all the silver still in existence, and then consolidating the bottom, lastly reforming and refashioning the base. The missing parts of silver had to be replaced, using the normal technique of silver soldering. A large dent which can be seen in the bottom right-hand half of the base was eradicated by first of all unscrewing the top half to get at the inside, and, using a former and working from the outside with a special smith's hammer to bring out the dent. (Plate No. 24 shows the piece complete again.) If untrained attempts are made to remove blemishes, to mend antique silver pieces, to remove dents, or to replace broken parts, an exquisite piece, can easily be almost completely ruined.

One of the oldest methods of decorating silver is termed niello. With this, the design is engraved deeply into the silver and then filled with a lead compound which forms an almost jet-black pattern on the silver ground. The origin of the process is of extreme antiquity. The writer Pliny records it back as far as ancient Egypt, and examples have been found from Mycenae dating back to 1,500 B.C. The niello method of decoration can sometimes be very difficult to see in a heavily tarnished or dirty piece of silver that might be picked up in an out-of-the-way sale. Therefore, if suspicion is aroused as to a certain piece having this type of decoration, extreme care should be used in the cleaning, or the whole may be lost. If there is any doubt, the dipping method of cleaning mentioned earlier should be avoided, and the cleaning attempted by the cautious use of very gentle metal powders such as jeweller's rouge mixed to a paste with methylated spirit and applied with small swabs of cotton wool which, for intricate parts may be twisted on to a matchstick. The jeweller's rouge may also be rubbed very delicately with the finger tip, into the piece. If this is done, it is advisable to protect the nails and cuticles; to do this rub into the fingers one of the lanolin barrier creams.

Electrum, which is an alloy of gold and silver, may be cleaned by the 'Silver Dip' method. If this is not possible because of its size or if it is used as an inlay for wood, it may have the dip applied by a swab of cotton wool. Again, of course, it must be thoroughly washed afterwards. If badly stained, tarnished or corroded, the gentle use of jeweller's rouge may be made.

In the case of very badly tarnished silver that will not respond to dip or other cleaning methods, a process that can produce results if used with extreme care is to brush the surface gently with a 15% solution of ammonium thiosulphate in a 1% solution of 'Lissapol'. This, of course, should be rinsed off as soon as it has done its work. The brush should also be rinsed off afterwards or corrosion of the metal ferrule will take place.

If the tarnish is overlaid with green corrosion, a 5% solution of citric acid may be applied. This should be done with extreme caution as it is liable to strip too far if not watched. Plenty of water should be at hand to restrain it, and the piece of silver should be treated in small areas at a time.

Gold very seldom needs any other cleaning than polishing with a soft cloth, piece of cotton wool or very soft leather. As with silver, care should be taken that the cleaning materials used are scrupulously clean and have no foreign bodies that can cause abrasive effects. This polishing of gold, silver, or, for that matter, any metal, is a task which needs concentration, for it is all too easy to put the polishing cloth down on the table, pick it up, and, inadvertently with it some grains of scratchy dust, and in a few moments the loving work of years can be removed, and with it the beautiful patina of age. If a piece of gold work does need cleaning, nothing stronger than a 2% solution of 'Lissapol' should be used. Again, it should be rinsed off thoroughly and polished with a clean cloth.

Gilding, such as ormolu, needs care in any cleaning process because the layer of gold can have worn extremely thin with age. If gentle polishing with cotton wool or a soft cloth will not suffice, a very dilute solution of nitric acid, down to 1%, can be gently tried and then immediately rinsed off. Ormolu also can be cleaned by gentle application of weak ammonia. This should be applied with a small piece of cotton wool, and if the application does not lift the tarnish and grime at once, the strength may be gradually increased. Great care should be taken that the ammonia does not get on to the surrounding wood. As for varnish and polish it is a strong solvent and will lift them away and damage the surface. Ormolu can become so discoloured that it will not react to ammonia, and the cleaning will then have to be done with cyanide. As this is a highly poisonous chemical to have in the home it is best to take the piece to a qualified restorer.

The use of dilute nitric acid or weak ammonia may also be tried cautiously on gold-leaf covered mirror frames or picture frames, but it should be pointed out that experiment should be made on a part of the frame underneath or towards the back that will not show. All too often, what looks like dirt on gold-leaf covered objects, such as frames and mirrors, is not dirt at all. Rather, it is the bole and glair and gesso showing through the gold-leaf which has, through age, become worn away. When you realize how thin gold-leaf is itself, it is amazing that its effect lasts as long as it does. In general, never try and touch-up a gold-leaf covered frame, mirror or piece of furniture by using bronze powder either in size or in cellulose lacquer. The effect is very liable to appear garish, however well it may be toned down with thin washes of raw and burnt umber afterwards. It is a better course to leave what remains, rather than to try and bring it to life in this manner.

Copper and its alloys have been used for centuries. The name copper is said to derive from Cyprus, where the Romans mined this metal. Its alloys—brass (when it is mixed with zinc), and bronze (when mixed with tin)—also date back to antiquity. Brass made its first appearance in late Roman times; bronze even earlier, going back to Ur of the Chaldees and to the Bronze Age itself. Like silver, copper can be tarnished by sulphur impurities in the air or with materials with which it comes in contact. Besides this, one of its greatest enemies is moisture, especially moisture with fresh air, which contains oxygen. This condition will oxidize copper very rapidly. At the outset the oxidization causes a very thin film to dull the polish, but if allowed to continue, the film can turn to a green deposit.

Copper can be cleaned by the dip electro-chemical method mentioned earlier for silver. This should be conducted with a certain amount of caution, a small piece being attempted first to ensure that it is completely safe. Again it should, of course, be completely and thoroughly rinsed and dried. Obstinate stains, tarnish or oxidization on copper utensils may be removed by one or other of the brass polishes that can be bought in the shops. The cleaning material should be watched for dust and dirt fragments, to prevent scratching.

With copper, bronze, and, to a lesser extent brass, one of the highly valued attractions of age is the patina. It is the subtle 'feeling' that one sees in the surface of the metal that for hundreds of years has slowly weathered and mellowed with the atmosphere, cleaning and use. To-day, this patina, where possible, should be preserved and not buffed away with coarse cleaning powders or rough methods. For delicate examples of copper and brass, for which the domestic powders are too strong, jeweller's rouge or one of the very, very fine cleaning powders might be used with paraffin. With cleaning brass and copper, if it is engraved, it is of first importance to keep the cleaning powder away from the

Plate 23. Badly damaged 18th
century English silver censer.

Plate 24. The censer shown
in Plate 23 repaired.

Plate 25. Corroded gilt-bronze dating from about 1,000 B.C.

Plate 26. Gilt-bronze buckle shown in Plate 25 after treatment.

ate 27. Heavily corroded bronze figure

Plate 28. The bronze figure in Plate 27
after treatment and lacquering.

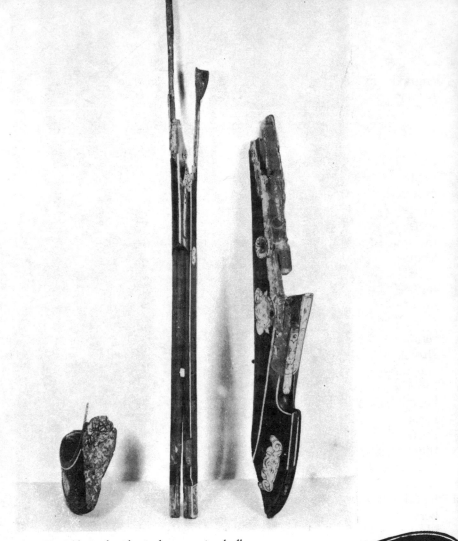

Plate 29. Old pistol with wooden mounting badly attacked by woodworm.

Plate 30. The pistol in Plate 29 after reconstructi

engraving, otherwise it will settle in the engraved lines and it will be very difficult to remove.

If brass, in particular, is badly corroded it may be cleaned with a very strong alkali such as washing soda solution, that is, sodium carbonate in water. One church, which has some lovely brass censers that become badly stained with incense and smoke, never hesitates actually to boil not only their censers but also brass candlesticks in a solution of sodium hydroxide about 5% to 7%. Then they are given a strong brushing with a burnishing brush, a special type of brush with very fine wire bristles. They should be thoroughly dried and then, like silver, they may if desired be lacquered. The best variety is probably ' Ercaline '.

Bronze has come down to us in many forms—beautiful statuettes and other objets d'art. It should be cleaned with the greatest care, because the beautiful patina of ancient bronze is a precious thing that should be preserved at all costs. If it is removed, the value of a piece will often melt away with it. Bronze has a special disease all its own, known as 'bronze disease', and this usually becomes evident as a bright green spot, which soon begins to spread. The ordinary well-known patina of rather beautiful greeny-blue is not bronze disease. This patina is a natural coating caused by the action of the air and atmosphere on the surface, which serves to preserve the metal alloy. But if tiny spots of bright bluish efflorescence appear in this greeny-blue patina, a condition is arising which must be attended to and, moreover, must not be attempted oneself. An expert should be called in at once. If this is not possible for a period of time, the best course is to gently brush off the loose efflorescence and then place the piece in as dry an atmosphere as possible; it is moisture which causes the disease to develop. Bronze may be lacquered but it is not a finish that will be found attractive for this material which owes its charm to the semi-matt surface of the patina. Bronze statues, if placed outside in the full effects of the weather and atmosphere, may need some protection, particularly on the coast where salt winds can reach them. This may be done by a thin coating of beeswax. Unbleached beeswax should be dissolved in turpentine heated in a double boiler; the wax should be cut up into small pieces and care with fire should be exercised. When the mixture is cool it should have the consistency of butter, and then it may be applied with brush or cloth to the bronze statue. The application should be repeated at intervals. The statue should, of course, be cleansed with warm water and a weak soap solution before applying the wax. To illustrate the extent to which a badly corroded object can be resuscitated and brought back to life, Plates 25 and 26 show a gilt-bronze buckle that probably dates from about 1,000 B.C. In this the corrosion has oozed through the gilt-work causing distortion in several places. After restoration it can be seen that in the hinge-top, the rivets are visible, and the shape and contour of the clasp has fully appeared. The treatment here was that the buckle was immersed in a solution of alkaline salts, which is the standard procedure for an object in this state. The solution was changed continuously as soon as the liquid became murky, and the corrosion was coming off. This took place probably once a day, and was continued until the gilt-work was clean and as much of the corrosion was removed as possible without damaging the base metal. Finally, the bronze buckle was immersed in a lacquer in this case 'Ercaline', to preserve it from further attacks from fumes and moisture in the air. A second example of the removal of corrosion from a bronze figure can be seen in Plates Nos. 27, 28. This is a small Chinese bronze figure dating from somewhere in the period between 1,000 B.C. and 900 A.D. The figure was so badly corroded that it was almost impossible to see the detail in the face and dress. The metal was gilt-bronze and it was given the same treatment as the bronze buckle: immersion in a solution of alkaline salts, finally being thoroughly washed in distilled water and then lacquered with 'Ercaline'.

Small statuettes are occasionally made from lead, and this same metal is sometimes employed for decorating balusters, legs of furniture and other pieces. Lead usually has a dull grey appearance. This is a natural oxidization which takes place by contact with the air; it is the lead's own patina, which is not only attractive but also protects the metal. Lead is one of the softest metals and, therefore, very prone to damage from the effects of hard polishing, scrubbing with a brush or inadvertent accident when moving. If the lead corrodes heavily a white incrustation makes its appearance, and this may be removed by careful application of a very weak solution of hydrochloric acid on small areas which is then washed off with an equally dilute solution of ammonium acetate. Lastly, it must be rinsed freely with plenty of clean water. The lead piece may be waxed after drying, if desired.

Oxidization can affect tin; it forms a greenish hue which may be cleaned in a similar manner to silver, electro-chemically or, if the oxidization or corrosion is obstinate, gentle physical cleaning with a fine powder such as jeweller's rouge.

Although tin is occasionally found in the form of jugs and plates, these are more often made of pewter, an alloy of lead and tin which at one time was used extensively for making domestic vessels of this type. Pewter, being made of these two metals, is soft and can almost be bent with the fingers. If it is dented or abraded, it should be handed to a metalsmith to correct the damage. Do not be tempted, with this or with any metalwork for that matter, to employ the old housewife's method of burnishing out a scratch or small dent, the effect is almost certain to be garish and out of character with the age of the piece, such treatment must be left to the expert. Pewter, like bronze, lead and other metals acquires a patina with age. The warm, dark shading in the crevices and moulding of the article is one of the chief attractions of this alloy. This appearance should be respected; for, if the pewter were to be chemically cleaned and come pristine from the bath, all its attraction would be lost. It is very important to avoid over-cleaning this metal. If the pewter piece will not 'come up' with a polishing cloth, a very mild abrasive, such as rotten-stone or crocus powder, may be applied with an oily rag; again, this must be done very gently and watching all the time that it is being carried out. After that, the polish may be cleaned away with a swab of cotton wool with a little methylated spirit and the article is then washed.

Old pewter, which started life centuries back, may sometimes have small, spot-like growths appearing on the surface. These are probably because of contamination with salts, and, if the spots are hard and show no active signs of corrosion, it is wisest not to try and polish them off or to abrade them. If this happens the underlayers of metal are exposed to the air and active fresh corrosion may take place.

Iron and steel objects such as statues, ornamental hinges, locks and armour are difficult problems, both from the point of view of protection and cleaning. Both iron and steel are readily attacked by rust, and once this has got a firm hold, it can be almost impossible to completely eradicate.

With burnished steel, rust which has not got a firm grip can be treated first by softening with paraffin oil for several hours, then worked over very carefully with an abrasive powder or paper, tackling a small area at one time. The difficulty with this kind of cleaning is to get an overall, even effect at the finish. It is all too easy to end up with a series of brightly shining blobs against the untreated part, Rust, in general, must be softened before being abraded away. A commercial product known as 'Plus-Gas Fluid "A" is an excellent softening agent and could be used in conjunction with a proprietary rust remover such as 'Jenolite'. The Plus-Gas fluid could be applied first, then removed, and an application of the Jenolite made. After the period of time suggested on the instructions with this latter fluid, gentle application of steel wool could be applied to remove the loosened rust. The trouble with rust, particularly when it is of long standing is that it tends to bite deeply into the metal, causing pitting. If this occurs, little can be done to remedy the defect.

In the keeping of iron and steel pieces in the home therefore, it is of paramount importance to watch the humidity and dampness of the rooms in which they are kept. In old houses where there may be a lack of a dampcourse, rising damp will very quickly affect any iron and steel objects, so that inspection should be made at fairly regular intervals. Look particularly at the back and the bottom of pieces if they are in positions similar to the above. The sulphur dioxide fumes of large towns also help to produce a condition which accelerates rusting.

If the pieces are in good condition and rust-free when purchased, or if it has been possible to remove the rust, it is wise to give the armour or other objects some kind of surface-protective treatment. This may be a cellulose lacquer, or, if you feel that the shiny surface obtained from this method is unaesthetic, the pieces can also be treated with lanolin, although the drawback to this is that the surface is liable to remain permanently sticky and, unless the object is in a case, it is impractical because of dust. A third layer protection can be of wax, which could be of beeswax and turpentine as was recommended for the bronze statue, a good furniture polish or microcrystalline wax polish. A wax coating may advantageously be placed over the cellulose lacquer as additional protection, and will reduce the gloss of the lacquer. A fourth protective coating can be prepared by using a mixture of vaseline and turpentine. The waxes, vaseline and lanolin should be sparingly applied with a swab of cotton wool.

The restoration of weapons, particularly guns, can be a complex matter if several different types of material have been used in the gun's manufacture—wood and metal having to be treated separately before reconstruction. Plates Nos. 29, 30, show the amount of treatment which was necessary with an old pistol that had been long neglected. Before work started, the wood had become very badly decayed, principally from attack by woodworm, almost the whole structure having been destroyed. This had to be reconstructed and consolidated with a permanent non-shrinking resin of the epoxy or polyester type. The metal-work then had to be treated for rust. Lastly, surface preservatives of lacquers or wax were applied after the whole had been reassembled.

Damascene work, which is often found on weapons of different kinds, needs particular care in cleansing as different metals are combined together. The damascene may be of the gold or silver wire on steel or iron, or it may be a type where different rods have been hammered and soldered into position which give a form of 'watered silk' appearance. With this second type of damascening, much of the beauty of the original craftsmanship is lost if the metal is allowed to become dull or even slightly rusty. One method of bringing up the damascene work, which can be carefully attempted, is to prepare a mixture of weak nitric acid with methylated spirit. It should be underlined that if you are attempting this it must be done near a plentiful supply of running water. Application should be made very sparingly with a swab of cotton wool. Watch it intently, as the nitric acid will have an etching result, and should only be applied for a few seconds and then the blade plunged under the water to sluice away the effect of the acid. This method can sometimes be successful in bringing back the pattern. After it has been carried out, the blade should be very thoroughly rinsed to remove all traces of the acid. It should then be dried and given either a wax or grease treatment similar to that in the previous paragraph on armour. It is most important once the wax or grease treatment has been completed, that there should be no stickiness of any kind; for if this is present, dust and abrasive particles may adhere to the blade, and as it is put into or pulled out of its scabbard damage can be caused to the delicate surface of the metal; therefore, one of the best waxes to use is the cream polish mentioned in the chapter on furniture.

This nitric acid and methylated spirit treatment can be given to the gold and silver damascene, but, again, with the very brief application and plentiful rinsing.

Iron and steel firedogs and baskets may be treated in the same way as armour. First the rust should be softened and removed as far as possible with one of the rust removing preparations, and then, if the fireplace is not to be used at all, or only during the winter months, it should have a protective coating similar to one of those suggested for armour.

Steel table knives are particularly prone to rust if they are in sporadic use. It is most important to make quite sure that the knives are properly dried when washing up, particularly after a large dinner. The cloths become dampened and may give the appearance of drying a knife blade by not leaving drops of water on it, but they can leave a general haze of moisture which can attack and cause rust if the knives are put away for two or three weeks before being used again. Earlier in this chapter suggestions were made for storing pieces which were not being used in thoroughly dried paper or in sealed polythene bags. Steel knives may also be treated with a weak grease-coating which could be quite simply removed with an adequate detergent before being used again. Steel knives in particular, become unsightly to use, if they are attacked by rust.

Copper coins, silver coins and medals of bronze, copper or silver, may be cleaned by immersing for a short period in a solution of 5% nitric acid. Again, this should be done under careful scrutiny, as the acid can etch into the metals, particularly the copper. It should be done first of all for a few seconds. The coin should then be removed, washed under a running tap or in plenty of fresh water, and examined, if necessary with a magnifying glass, to see whether the metal is actually being attacked. If the coins have patches of corrosion, or heavy tarnish exhibited, the exposed metal may first be covered with a wax or grease film to protect it from the acid. This treatment can succeed in quite obstinate cases. After removal of the deposits, the coins should be thoroughly washed and then treated with either the lanoline grease or with cream wax polish.

In all the suggestions for treatment for the various metals in this chapter, it should be underlined once more that it is very important indeed, where a solvent or acid is being used, that it should be thoroughly sluiced away before any protective coat such as grease, wax or lacquer is applied. If this is not done, the corrosive action of the solvent or acid will be sealed in and can continue its work, often with disastrous results. This washing away is particularly necessary with elaborate metal chasing or scrolling work with deep corners and crevices. It can be assisted by application of a weak detergent which should itself be washed away with plenty of warm water. Lastly, with any of the metals mentioned here, before any protective treatment, they must be thoroughly and completely dried. Adequate supplies of really dry cloths, dried out cotton wool, should be available. With deep chasing or complicated scrolling and depth of modelling, the pieces could be even better safeguarded by a period in an efficient airing cupboard or really warm room. The airing cupboard, if used, should of course have been cleared of clothes, towels or sheets that have come back from the laundry, otherwise it could be a danger spot, as the atmosphere would be moist and warm which could be even more effective in causing rust or tarnish.

Metals such as lead or pewter that are particularly susceptible to the action of acid should not be stored in drawers or cupboards of oak, because of the volatile acid given off by the wood.

With all badly damaged metal objects pitted or scratched, whether of silver, copper, iron, steel or whatever kind, it is a question for advice and treatment by a qualified professional restorer. Never should any fierce treatment in the way of abrasion or over-strong solvents and acids be used, as many of the metals which are of antiquity can be frail. They are very liable to attack and this could considerably damage them and, in bad cases, render them almost impossible to reclaim or repair. Even some cleaning liquids can quite speedily affect sensitive patinas. Once these attractive sheens of age have gone or been partly removed, there is no way of exactly reproducing the appearance which took many, many years to achieve.

3 Glass, Ceramics, Bone, Ivory and Jewellery

EUROPE IS RICH IN CENTRES THAT HAVE IN THE PAST AND still do produce fine glass. To-day's well-formulated soda glass and stable glass like 'Pyrex' are relatively free from attack from most sources. But the glass, prior to the 17th century, made from silica, lime, soda or potash, can be affected quite severely by humidity. One of the signs of deterioration in these earlier glasses is an opalescence, a pearl-like reflective quality appearing in the material. This can be seen in an advanced state on some examples of Roman glass in collections and museums. With the antique glasses of this nature, another condition may arise which is known as 'weeping glass'. This happens when too large a percentage of alkali is present, a large amount of potassium salts which are hygroscopic; the weeping is caused by drops of potassium carbonate, a very strong alkali, running down the glass. Treatment for this is a matter for the specialist, and the glass should be transferred to his laboratory as soon as possible.

Even contemporary glass can be affected if exposed for a long time in very damp conditions. The storing of any glass should be in as dry conditions as possible. When put away, glass should never be wrapped in tissue or other paper as this can harbour damp, and it should always be in cupboards or on shelves where there is adequate ventilation; stagnant air will generally be consonant with dampness.

Glass begins to break down when exposed to extreme humidity. The glass itself can absorb moisture on to its surface. If it is a potash glass, carbon dioxide will also be absorbed from the atmosphere, which produces the condition of 'weeping' mentioned in a previous paragraph. The reaction will not be so quick with soda glass.

When washing glass, the water should not be too hot. The water can contain a weak detergent, and each piece should be washed separately. Needless to say, the washing bowl should never be piled with a dozen or more pieces of glass. Rinsing should be with cold water although with frail specimens the change of temperature should be gradual. The piece should then be dried with a soft linen cloth; or an old soft chamois leather. Cotton cloths are not suitable as they leave pieces of fluff on the glass.

Glass, strictly speaking, should not stain—it is non-porous—but decanters in particular, when bought at sales, often show an opaque cloudiness on the inside. There are two causes for this: either the remains of wine or dampness. If it is the first, the wine deposits can be removed fairly simply with a mild acid such as 5% sulphuric or nitric acid. The decanter, after this treatment, should be rinsed out half a dozen times or more with clean water. If it is the second, it means that the decanter has been repeatedly left damp, and the glass on the surface of the interior has literally broken down from being subjected to over-humidity.[6]

To dry a decanter out properly, it should be left to drain upside-down overnight. A drying-cloth should then be insinuated into it and rubbed round. If it is being put into store, never leave it with the stopper in; leave the stopper beside it. To keep dust or particles from the inside, put a paper handkerchief, which is porous, over the top and keep it in place with a rubber band. Another way which could be used to dry out a decanter is to use the low heat from a hair-dryer.

To mend breaks in glass is a most difficult task, as the joins are almost certain to show unless they are conveniently along a cut or engraving in the glass. Different types of adhesives will give reasonable results: these include 'Araldite 101', 'Araldite 103' (these two should not be used for valuable specimens) and 'Durofix'. If you want to make your own adhesive, an excellent one

[6] See Appendix.

is made by dissolving pieces of Perspex in glacial acetic acid 5 ml., with ethylene dichloride 195 ml. If the glass has suffered a multi-break and it is desired to build up the bowl, drinking glass or other complicated piece, it assists to hold the fragments in place while the mend is going on if they are backed with adhesive tape. The sticky tape can be gently pulled off when the adhesive has dried, and if any stickiness remains it can be removed by gently wiping, very quickly, with either methylated spirit or acetone.

An illustration of the building up and final repair of a piece of glass can be seen in Plates Nos. 31, 32, 33. These are fragments of an Indian enamelled green glass bottle. It can be noticed how, as the build up is carried through, the pieces are kept aligned by the use of temporary patches and strips of adhesive paper outside the bottle. The fragments throughout are held in position by the internally applied strips of epoxy resin which have been reinforced by a thin, fibrous veil of glass-fibre. The purpose of this was that this type of mat becomes transparent when embedded in resin; this will therefore keep any alteration to the translucence of the glass bottle to the minimum.

Stained glass usually keeps its brilliance and splendid colours for a very long period without needing attention, but certain conditions can cause deposits and fogging of the surface. Undue over-humidity plus fumes from heating appliances such as coal-fires or gas-fires can cause these conditions. The remedy is comparatively simple: the glass areas should be washed over with 5% solution of ammonia in distilled water. The liquid is best applied with a brush which can be gently scrubbed round on the surface of the glass until the deposit is rinsed off. The glass should then be washed to rid it of all the solvent. Care should be exercised, however, particularly if the window was executed during the last 50 years of the 19th century. Much of this Victorian glass was poorly fired and the colour was not fused properly into the surface of the glass. The same thing applies to the shading colour and the tracing, as this 5% solution of ammonia can, if left on any length of time, remove much of both of these.

Mould forms may appear on stained glass in churches or buildings where there is very excessive humidity, or with rising damp in walls. This can also be removed with ammonia, and, after being rinsed and dried, could be wiped over with a sparing amount of 'Santobrite' in a 5% solution to protect it from further attack. In Plate No. 34 can be seen a fragment of one of the windows in the William Morris room, formerly called The Green Dining Room, in The Victoria and Albert Museum in London. This shows the full extent of the deposit which was supposedly caused by fumes from a cooking-stove which stood too close to the windows before the war. In Plate No. 35 can be seen the same portion with the cleaning away of the deposit commenced.

Some of the most beautiful pieces of jewellery and plaques have been produced by enamelling. Enamel is only a coloured glass; a lead-glass to which some metallic oxide has been added to give it a colour or to make it opaque and give it a tint. It is applied thinly on to a metal base which can be copper or other base metals, or on to gold and silver. This glass is then infused on to the metal; therefore, changes of heat are particularly dangerous for enamels of any kind. They should not be kept in a window where direct sunlight can fall upon them as temperature can obviously cause a considerable internal strain to be set up as the glass is fused directly on to the metallic backing and this strain is increased by temperature changes. Further, if the enamel is on a metal like copper, overhumidity and dampness must be avoided, as moisture can activate acids and salts and may cause the copper to corrode and this may lift the enamel.

If the enamel becomes crazed or loose, almost the only course that is open is to attempt to reattach it by covering freely with either Bedacryl 122X or a lacquer such as 'Frigilene'. After this has soaked right in and dried off, excess lacquer can be removed from the actual surface of the enamel by careful wiping with a well wrung out swab of cotton wool that has been dipped in acetone.

Cleaning of a dirty enamel can best be done with lukewarm water and a good soft soap with possibly a little ammonia. The application should be made with a small paint brush; this can gently scrub the surface and interstices.

Fungus or mould growths can sometimes be observed on top or in between the colours of old enamels, which show evidence of slight cracking and previous damage. What has probably happened here is that earlier the piece was damaged and the fragments were reset with an animal glue such as Scotch or rabbit's-skin. This mould or fungus is started by bacteria taking root in the adhesive. The best treatment is to wipe the affected part with a 2% solution of 'Santobrite' and after this has dried, apply the lacquer treatment mentioned above.

The cleaning of hard-fired porcelain, Oriental porcelain or stoneware is comparatively easy, as these are all non-porous and will not absorb water or other materials. Before starting, however, the pieces should be carefully inspected for cracks or imperfections in the glaze, and if they are of considerable value, they should be treated separately. The water should not be too hot, and any of the detergents which are safe for use with your hands are suitable. The pieces should be rinsed in clean water to remove the detergents, and then well dried afterwards.

Faience and pottery should not be completely immersed in water, but should be gently cleansed with a damp rag. Where metal mountings are included, the porcelain part of the piece should be washed with a damp rag to which detergent may be added, and the metal should be treated separately. This may range from gold or gilded copper to pewter and other metals. The cleaning of these should be carried out as by the instructions in Chapter II on Metals.

Staining in tea or coffee-cups often detracts from the pieces, and this can be tackled if great care is employed. In the 18th century, some of the pieces produced were unstable, particularly if they were decorated with coloured glaze which had been fused on to the surface. A strong bleach applied to a piece of Chelsea Ware, for example, could severely damage it, the decoration coming away. But, generally speaking, a bleach such as hydrogen peroxide should be reasonably safe to use with white pieces. Experiment should be made on a small portion at a time, using the bleach in increasing strength until the desired result is effected.

Before starting any rigorous treatment, the value of the piece should be carefully considered against the possible damage that can be done to it. If there is any doubt, professional advice should be taken.

The repair of broken pieces of porcelain, earthenware or terracotta, is difficult, because unless the joint is got back to a hair-line, the pieces will never go together again correctly and there will always be some distortion. Therefore, the adhesives chosen should be of a thin variety. Before a repair is made, the pieces to be put back should be examined for dirt and dust, and if the break was made a long time ago they should be carefully cleansed with some kind of degreasing detergent to make sure that the surface of the pieces are absolutely clean. If this is not done it will be impossible to make an effective repair. On the market there are a wide variety of modern synthetic resin adhesives from which a choice can be made. One point before starting the mend is to remember that many of these adhesives are indissoluble once set, so that the repair should be as exact as you can make it.

Sometimes, a piece may be purchased in a sale which has been badly mended. It may be advisable to undo the mend and repair it again. The types of glue that were used before the war can be dissolved. Between the two wars the glues used may have been of the 'Durofix' type and these dissolve in acetone. Small cotton wool pads of this liquid can be held on each side of the crack until the glue gives way. Prior to the First World War, and certainly before 1900, the glues will probably be animal and these can be broken down by holding swabs of cotton wool soaked in hot water on each side of the mend. If not of animal substance the adhesive might have been shellac, and this can be removed by swabs of cotton wool dipped in methylated spirit.

The repair of a piece of porcelain, stoneware or earthenware can be a first-class jig-saw puzzle in three dimensions. In Plate No. 36 can be seen the shattered remains of a German stoneware jug. This had been fired in a reducing atmosphere and decorated with cobalt and manganese. This particular piece had originally been repaired by using Canada balsam which had become brittle and the piece fell to bits almost at the touch. Inside, it had been originally strengthened by the use of old book-boards and paper, which had been stuck in place with a compound of resin, beeswax and whiting. Before starting, the balsam and resin adhesive all had to be removed, all the joints degreased and thoroughly cleaned. The difficulty with this specific piece was the considerable size of the pot, and the fact that the walls in some places were less than $\frac{1}{8}''$ thick. It had apparently been made in two parts and then roughly welded together by hand. The build-up for a piece in this condition was a laborious process. One of the modern synthetic resin-adhesives suitable for stoneware or porcelain was used, and internal strengthening of glass-fibre was applied as the piece mounted up. In this particular instance, the restoration is shown in Plate No. 37 almost complete. The patches missing will have to be built up, using a resin such as 'Araldite CY 219' mixed with a substance such as marble flour, silica flour, slate powder or vermiculite. This should be modelled up as near as possible to the surrounding patterning and design. The pattern is, generally, more or less repetitive, with pieces similar to this; therefore, simulation is comparatively easy. Colour may be applied when the filling material has set; probably the best would be egg-tempera or an artist's good oil colour. If you are using tempera, care would have to be taken over the tonal change when the surface lacquer is applied, as many of the colours may darken considerably. As far as possible, avoid any touching-in which goes over the original glaze. When the in-painting colours have dried out thoroughly, the surface can be lacquered or varnished with a synthetic resin varnish.

Terra-cotta figures or pieces should be cleaned with the minimum of liquid. The best course is to first dust carefully with a soft brush, and where dust accumulates in fine details of the modelling it can be lightly dusted with whiting or very mild abrasive powder in an attempt to loosen the grime. If this fails, a mild detergent can be applied again with the brush and rinsed off as soon as possible. If desired, terra-cotta can be given a matt polish, and this will also give it a protective coat against dirt in the atmosphere. The cream polish is suitable for this and should be put on as sparingly as possible and then buffed-up with pieces of cotton wool which have been dipped lightly in finely powdered French chalk.

Ivory is a material which has been used for carved pieces, knife-handles, piano-keys and it often attains a yellowish tone. It should be realized that the yellowing, or natural patination of ivory, is the result of time, and is not necessarily a defect. Unless it is very displeasing, the wisest course is to leave it alone, but if bleaching is desired it can be done by coating the surface of the ivory with a stiff paste of whiting and 20 volume hydrogen peroxide. When doing this, rubber gloves should be worn. The object should be coated uniformly with this paste, which should not be too wet and the operation should be done on a dry day, so that if possible it can be stood outside in the sun afterwards. Ivory behaves some-what similarly to wood in its reaction to moisture, and is likely to warp and crack if it swells unevenly. You should, therefore, be careful not to use too much water when using this paste, and the object should be propped up so that all the main surfaces are exposed to the air. The paste should be carefully washed off after treatment, and the object immediately dried with a soft cloth, Lastly, as a protective coating, a very small amount of almond oil can be applied; this will also restore the soft shine.

Ivory and bone are both easily affected by heat, which can cause distortion and warping. Applications of water should also be kept at a minimum. Surface cleaning of ivory or bone, however, may be carried out with warm water and a mild detergent, preferably done with a piece of cotton wool or soft cloth which has been dipped into the liquid, and well wrung out. Rinsing should be carried out with the minimum of liquid and the pieces should be thoroughly dried as soon as possible.

When carrying out a repair on broken ivory or bone pieces, adhesives such as 'Durofix', isinglass or one prepared from white shellac, would be appropriate.

One of the most commonly occurring sins of washing–up is that bone or ivory-handled knives are immersed in water, or even left standing in jugs of over-hot water with just the blades immersed, here the steam and moisture can penetrate the highly susceptible handles and adhesive which is used to bind the steel and handle together. Before 1900 this certainly would have been of an animal composition, and therefore easily loosened. Good bone-handled knives, and certainly ivory-handled knives, should be washed individually, and moisture kept away from the handle and the seating of the blade into the handle. If it becomes loosened, the steel spike of the blade should be carefully cleaned of old adhesive, and, as far as possible the old adhesive removed from the hole in the handle. This can be carried out with a knitting needle wrapped round with lint or cotton wool. The handles can be refixed with 'Durofix' or one of the synthetic glues. If they fit too loosely, the glue can be mixed into a paste with marble dust or fine whiting. This is then fed into the hole in the handle and the spike of the blade forced into it.

Staining in ivory or bone is a difficult problem. Owing to the nature of the material it generally goes right through and does not remain on or near the surface. If the method described previously of applying hydrogen peroxide and whiting, does not suffice, advice should be taken. This particularly applies to fine ivory pieces which may have had burnt-staining or colour-staining applied when made. When carving pieces of netsuke, the Japanese often employed artificial colouring.

If the ivory carving or piece is of considerable age and value, it would be wiser to use a mixture of water and a little methylated spirit instead of using water alone, as this will cause the moisture to evaporate more rapidly. Again, if the grime is obstinate, a little powdered whiting mixed with methylated spirit might be gently applied on a small swab of cotton wool, or cotton wool round a matchstick. This may also help to overcome residual darkness in the crevices and cracks that may be impossible to wash out and clean completely as the whiting will tend to form up in the crack and take on the colour of its surround. When the dirt has been removed from the ivory, dry it out with a soft, absorbent cloth. It may then be treated with almond oil or a very fine coat of microcrystalline can be applied. This will not only act as a protective, but will also bring up the finish of the carving.

Tortoise-shell and horn are used considerably for inlay work, occasionally for carving, and also for the lids of small patch-boxes or trinket-boxes. If these become grimed or dirty, they may be washed with soap and warm water, using a pure soap such as Lux, or a liquid mild detergent. The method should be to use small swabs of cotton wool dipped into the water and soap or detergent and wrung out so that a minimum amount of moisture gets on to the piece. They should be rinsed off using plenty of swabs that have been dipped in clean water and wrung out in the same manner. They may be finished by using a light wax polish; here again the cream polish is most suitable. Repairs should be carried out with a thin adhesive such as 'Durofix' or one of the synthetic resins. Specimens of horns in trophies often flake or start to split from the ends that go into the animal's head. This can be reinforced by placing plastic tapes or thin bandage material stuck into place with a resin glue, inside the base of the horn.

The cleaning of substances which have been inlaid with mother of pearl, shell or coral, should be undertaken very gently. No solvent with any kind of acid in it should be employed as this will attack these materials. Cotton wool swabs with weak detergent that have been well wrung out should be sufficient to remove grime, but careful rinsing must be carried out afterwards. If this method is not sufficient gentle abrasion with a swab of cotton

Plate 31. Fragments of an Indian enamelled green glass bottle.

Plate 32. Building up the bottle in Plate 31
showing use of temporary paper strips and
fibrous glass reinforcement.

Plate 33. Repairs complete to
the Indian bottle.

Plate 34. Stained glass covered in moulds, from William Morris room.

Plate 35. The same fragment in Plate 34 with treatment being carried out.

Plate 36. Fragments of a German
stoneware jug.

Plate 37. The same jug shown in
Plate 36 with repairs almost complete.

wool dipped in fine whiting or powdered pumice may be tried. After this has been cleaned off, the surface can be polished with wax cream.

Amber beads, or small carvings in this material, often accumulate grime and dirt owing to the soft nature of their surface. Under no circumstances should they ever be cleaned off with any spirit solvent, even as mild as turpentine substitute, as the amber which is a fossilized resin can be dissolved with this type of liquid. Cleaning should be by washing with warm water and a mild soap or detergent. In excessive coatings, the swabs of cotton wool can again be dipped into a very mild abrasive powder such as French chalk, the amber afterwards being treated by buffing-up with a soft chamois.

Jewellery, the moulding and settings of precious and semi-precious stones into metals, should be treated very circumspectly. If a claw setting has not been employed, the adhesives may vary widely and can easily be attacked and the stones loosened. Generally speaking, the cleaning should not be anything further than dusting with a small brush or buffing-up very gently with a soft, old chamois leather. If the setting is mechanical and there is no adhesive or plaster-type setting used, the pieces can be gently cleansed. This can be with warm water and mild detergent, using a small brush, and followed by plentiful rinsing; finally drying on a soft cloth or chamois leather. In obstinate cases methylated spirit could be applied, again with a brush, but if the piece is of extreme value or there is any doubt as to its condition a professional jeweller should be consulted.

Eau de Cologne can be used in the same way, and sometimes may penetrate and loosen accretions of grime more quickly. If possible, carry out the cleaning using a jeweler's eye-glass or under some other type of magnification. Never force the head of the brush into the setting; use the hairs gently to 'tease out' rather than 'force out' the dirt.

4 *Marble, Stone and Sculpture*

SCULPTURE AND CARVING IN STONE, WHETHER MARBLE, limestone, sandstone or igneous rocks such as basalt and granite, are by no means immune from attacks either by decay from atmosphere or fungi. The problem will differ depending on whether they are outside or inside the building.

Articles of stone outside have to contend with wind and rain, and, in the winter harsh temperature changes from frost and snow. They may also (by their situation) be attacked by mildew. They can further be affected by sulphur fumes in the air. Indoors, most stones are affected by these same sulphur impurities from fires and other sources, to a more or less degree. They can also become stained from liquids spilt on them and, with carved mantelpieces and similar articles, a common cause of damage is from spilt candlewax.

The cleaning of the igneous rocks which are extremely hard and almost completely non-porous, can be fairly rigorous without damage. If carvings or monuments of granite or basalt are obscured under centuries of grime, smoke and soot, they can be scrubbed with stiff bristled and, even wire bristled brushes without damage. Sometimes the layer of grime may be so obstinate that detergent will not penetrate it, and a solvent made up of 9 parts carbon tetrachloride*mixed with 1 part benzene, may be applied, but this should be first mixed with 1% of 'Lissapol N' to form an

*This substance is highly poisonous and full ventilation should be provided and great care taken not to inhale it.

emulsion. Needless to say, the stone should be liberally washed for about half-an-hour after the application of a solvent such as this, to make quite certain that all traces of the solvent are removed. After it has been allowed to dry, the surface could be treated with a 10% solution of paraffin wax dissolved in turpentine substitute. About two hours after the application of the wax has been made, the surface of the block of stone should be gently warmed with a small electric stove or blow-lamp to temporarily melt the wax and make quite sure that it has impregnated the surface of the stone thoroughly into cracks and softer areas.

Although much softer than the igneous rocks, limestone and sandstone tend, with time, to form a protective layer or patina. Quite severe damage may ensue if this is disturbed by over-hard cleaning, as underneath the immediate surface can be quite soft and porous, almost in a powdery state.

Darkening by soot deposits and other impurities in limestone can best be treated with a prolonged application of running fresh water, but first of all care should be taken to examine the piece thoroughly so as to make certain that it is not a composition, a fake or replacement in other material. The clean water can be played freely over the piece with hoses of reasonably high pressure. The treatment should be maintained for a long period: up to six hours will not hurt. Occasionally, the spraying can be interrupted so that the grime can be loosened with a stiff bristled brush charged with a weak ammonia solution, about 5%. Under no condition should any cleansing, abrasive powders be used.

The cleaning of blemishes from mildew stains or other causes is best carried out by using paper pulp. The method is that a cheap grade of soft white paper should be heated in distilled water and then given a thorough beating in a bowl until it is reduced to a pulp. Newspaper with print on it should not be used, for quite obvious reasons. When the pulp has cooled, a layer of it about $\frac{1}{2}''$ to $\frac{3}{4}''$ thick should be laid over the blemish or stain and left. What happens is that first of all the moisture from the pulp sinks into the stone, loosening the stain, and then, as evaporation takes place, the moisture with the impurities is drawn out of the stone and into the paper pulp. This same pulp treatment can be applied to an oil stain or wax. In this case, the pulp should be dried completely to rid it of water content, and then soaked in a mild solvent, such as turpentine substitute. It is then placed over the stain or wax deposit in a similar way as the first example. With wax deposit, any surface lumps of wax may first of all be chipped or cut away to hasten the result. If the turpentine solvent is not strong enough, pure turpentine might be used or turpentine substitute mixed with industrial methylated spirit or acetone, gradually increasing the strength as necessary.

Marble, with its high finished texture, particularly if it is of a white or a light tone, is very susceptible to staining from mildew or rust, and to surface-layer contamination from smoke, fumes, dirt and dust in the household or outside air. For general light cleaning, a high quality soap may be used with clean warm water. If this does not prove strong enough, half a teacupful of ammonia can be added to a bucketful of clean water, and the surface of the marble should be brushed with a rotary motion, working quite a small patch at a time, and thoroughly rinsing with clean water before moving on to the next. The surface should be carefully dried with a clean white cotton rag or ample supplies of cotton wool. White marble is very easily discoloured, and every effort must be made to ensure that coloured soaps, cloths with colours that can run or rusty buckets are not employed. One further point is that the piece should be carefully dusted free of all loose dirt before starting, otherwise abrasive material may be left which will be scratched into the surface when the washing takes place. It is not advisable to use cleaning powders or pastes as they can easily damage the fine surface of the marble. If the piece is standing out of doors and has any holes or cracks, these should be filled in before the winter to prevent damage from frost and ice. A local mason can advise as to the best materials to use.

The danger of staining for white and light coloured marbles cannot be over-emphasized. When damp is present, anything with colour in it can all too easily transmit a stain onto the stone. Packing materials, straw, corrugated paper, are culprits; even white, clean cloths, if damp and encouraging fungoid growth, can transmit this form of damage. The staining is often extremely difficult, almost impossible, to remove. One bleaching agent which may be employed is a very weak solution of 'Chloramine T' broken down to about 2%. It must, of course, be thoroughly rinsed off after use. If the stain resists this treatment, exposure to air and sunlight may bleach the stain away. This will also help to evaporate it if it is of a volatile nature. One further step that might be attempted after use of the 'Chloramine T' is the gentle application of very dilute hydrogen peroxide with a drop or two of ammonia. Again, thorough washing after the treatment is necessary.

Fly-marks, as with many other materials, are troublesome and unsightly. They can be removed from marble or other hard stone by gentle physical action, and the residue carefully wiped away with a little powdered whiting or precipitated chalk mixed with dilute ammonia. Generally speaking, no abrasive agent, such as emery or sandpapers, should be used on marble surfaces or other stones as this must inevitably damage the patina.

Slate-engraved tablets can be cleaned in the same manner as marble, the engraved portions being gently treated with cotton wool on a small sliver of wood.

Marble and slate when cleansed do not necessarily need any further treatment, but, if desired, a gentle polish may be given with a white wax. This can be prepared by dissolving beeswax in pure turpentine. In a dusty atmosphere this will afford useful protection against spoilage, and the wax may be quite simply removed by rubbing over with turpentine, at the same time bringing the surface dirt with it.

Sometimes monuments of marble include Coats of Arms which are painted, and one of the best ways to clean the paint areas is by the use of saliva. This should be applied with a cotton wool swab. Unless the paint is loose, you can rub quite vigorously. Human saliva contains a 'surface active agent' which acts in its own way, as a natural detergent. For touching-in, oil colours are not satisfactory. It is much better to employ egg-tempera colours. You can mix these by the traditional method if you have the time, using egg-yolk and dry pigments, but it is simpler to buy them ready-made in the tube. During the past 30 years these have been introduced by Rowney's and are completely satisfactory. If part of the paint is missing and the surface needs to be made up level before painting, this can be put back with 'Brummer' Stopping. To restore the gloss after the tempera colours have dried out, a synthetic varnish may be applied and, when this has hardened after twenty-four hours, a layer of fine cream wax polish should be put on which will reduce the gloss of the varnish and bring the surface sheen more in line with the marble.

For repair to marble, the best type of adhesive to use is one of the epoxy resin group such as 'Araldite'. This takes twenty-four hours to harden, and, during this time, the two parts of the piece being mended should be securely tied or clamped together. Other glues that can be employed if you require a quick setting adhesive, are polyvinyl acetate emulsion, 'Durofix' or 'Evostick'. For large repairs 'Tritone' should be used, or 'Sintolit'.

In Plate No. 38 may be seen an example of marble cleaning similar to that which has to be done at moderately frequent intervals, particularly if in a town atmosphere. The example on the left is before treatment with soft soap, ammonia and water, and on the right can be seen just how much dirt can be removed safely by this method.

For treatment of green algae or mildew stains, whether out-of-doors or from damp conditions indoors, the piece should be washed with solutions of chlorophenol or 'Santobrite'[4].With the last, a 5% solution would be satisfactory, and this will also give a reasonable, lasting protection to the piece. This particular product is one of the most effective anti-mildew or fungicide protectives. Mildew stains should be treated with the soft soap and ammonia method, or if this does not prove efficacious, the paper pulp applications can be made. As a protective treatment for statuary outside, waxing can be carried out in a similar manner to the procedure suggested for the igneous rocks earlier in this chapter. Perhaps a better method of application is to warm the stone first; before this is attempted it should be thoroughly dry and the warmth may be applied by standing or fixing an electric stove about 3 or 4 feet from the stone's surface. When it has been thoroughly warmed through, white beeswax, melted with white spirit can be applied. The consistency should be similar to soft butter, and care should be taken that no surplus is left on the surface of the statue after application. The reason for warming the stone is of course to draw the wax thoroughly into the immediate surface. Beeswax may tend to bring down the tone of the stone, and unless wiped off very thoroughly, it can cause accumulation of dirt. The fine cream polish may be used on stone with the better result, as it is not so sticky and will not affect the aesthetic effect to such an extent. For stone pieces that are outside, it would be unwise to apply a coating of lacquer, but, if the objects are indoors, lacquer brushed on will give a satisfactory protection. One form can be white shellac dissolved in methylated

4. See materials

spirit, rather similar to a type of French polish, also the proprietary product 'Bedacryl 122X' is suitable.

The replacement, or rather fabrication, of missing parts of antique sculpture or, for that matter, sculpture of any period is something that should not be done. It is not possible to simulate the technique and genius of artists from the past to the extent that an arm, leg, or part of the face can be happily replaced. Apart from this, any reconstruction carried out with plasters or cements will become quite obvious with the passage of time, however well they may be concealed under chalking or other surface treatments. The replacing of a broken piece is another matter and that has been described earlier.

One of the most frequently misunderstood materials is alabaster and, regrettably, many fine pieces in this delightful material have suffered from this lack of knowledge and destructive cleaning. Alabaster is a soft material and somewhat susceptible to water, particularly tap water, which can have dissolved acids in it. Therefore, any washing with soap and water should be kept to a minimum, particularly as the material itself is porous and may, where extremely soft, be almost soluble. If soap and water are used, the piece should be wiped over with a modest amount of liquid.

Normally, the dirt that gets ingrained into alabaster is of a greasy nature. First attempts to remove this should be a gentle exploratory wiping with white spirit. If this does not remove the grime, one or other of the domestic paint solvents may be employed. This, of course, should be rinsed away afterwards with the white spirit. Whether you wash with soap and water or a little detergent, white spirit, paint cleaner or petrol, experiment should be made on a small area first.[7] To replace chips on a work of alabaster, the mixture should ideally be alabaster dust or powdered gypsum and an adhesive such as 'Durofix'. If the alabaster dust or powdered gypsum cannot be procured, refined whiting may be used instead. The aim should be to make the mixture in such a way that it imitates the translucence of the particular area of the alabaster concerned. It may be found that the mixture will shrink and, therefore, the mend will have to be built up in layers. Final treatment should be to polish the alabaster with a sparing amount of beeswax dissolved in turpentine.

[7] See Appendix.

Where a piece of alabaster has been previously mended with animal or fish glue, the joints will almost inevitably have become dark brown with time, and unsightly. This glue should be removed, and to do this, small pads of cotton wool soaked in hot water should be left over the mend for a period of time. This treatment will eventually soften the glue, and the piece can then be removed, the sides of the joint wiped clean of the animal or fish glue with hot water. If staining remains after the washing, it may be gently swabbed with warm water containing about 20% of ammonia. When doing this, always work on a small area at a time, and test the result by letting the area dry out and polishing it to the same extent as the unstained ground. This is important, because it may look lighter when dried and before polishing, than it does after polishing. If the stain is obstinate, leave the ammonia swab on the area for up to an hour, and observe the result. If the ammonia is not strong enough to bleach out the stain, a similar treatment may be carried out with the proprietary liquid 'Milton', a chlorine bleach which should be sufficient. When making application of the bleach or ammonia, do not let the swabs of cotton wool be too soggy. Wring them out before applying them. It is most important not to let the liquids get on to any other part of the piece.

Plaster casts or small relief medallions in plaster can need treatment as with anything else, but extreme care is necessary with this friable material; it is extremely absorbent and delicate. Plaster casts or reliefs should first of all be completely dried, and may then be cleaned by brushing with a round hog's-hair brush charged with dry plaster of Paris, alternatively, a mixture of equal parts of 'Triple O' pumic powder and precipitated chalk. Care should be taken to avoid blunting any sharp relief detail.

Plaster casts are often coloured or treated to make them represent bronze. This may be done by painting over with a shellac varnish to which has been added Vandyke brown or burnt umber, with an addition of a green earth powder colour, the highlights being picked out with bronze powder either rubbed in or applied with cellulose or varnish. Alternatively, some small pieces may be treated with dark bronze powders and then be shade-treated with burnt umber, raw umber and other colours, to simulate the shadow and patina of a real bronze.

Sculpture is also made from other materials including different woods, wax and fired clays. The wooden pieces, often if they are of antiquity, were originally polychrome. In Plate No. 39 can be seen an example of polychrome sculpture which might be discovered or bought at a sale, and in Plate No. 40 can be seen the same piece after cleaning, the dirt removed, and before the replacement of the feet of the child and the left arm. In polychrome sculpture, restoration is difficult because it is sometimes almost impossible to find out what the original colours were. These kind of sculptures were frequently repainted, different colours being added, the repaints left in position, and, probably, they did not refer at all to the original colour scheme; in fact, in the first place the piece may have been covered in gold leaf. With a piece such as this, worm-holes and blemishes in the original paint are normally not restored. The treatment is much less than one would make with an oil painting, partly because the shape and form of the article is still preserved. As a result, quite a considerable amount of damage can be tolerated on the surface. If the restoration was taken too far and too high a degree of perfection of surface treatment reached, the whole feeling of age and truth would disappear. Cleaning off grime from a wooden carving such as this may be attempted by the use of solvents. In the first place, using cotton wool, wipe it with turpentine substitute to see how much the greasy grime of years will come away with this treatment. Often, quite an amount will be brought away, perhaps even enough for you to judge the condition of the surface underneath, or the colours you will be bringing up. Stronger solvents could include turpentine by itself, or a little methylated spirit mixed with the turpentine substitute or acetone with the turpentine substitute. If either of these latter solvents are used, they should be completely removed with turpentine substitute before the piece is left. Again, it should be emphasized that a very small area should be attempted first when using solvents as strong as these two, using a matchstick with cotton wool wrapped round it, and working on a part of the sculpture not readily visible. After treatment, when the piece has been cleaned, it should not be varnished, but rather waxed, an application of the fine cream polish being given. This will not only produce a harmonious sheen, but also act as a protective layer.

Wax figures are probably the most prone of any kind to damage from cleaning methods. If possible, these should be restricted to very gentle brushing with a soft haired paint brush, and, if obstinate types of grime persist, the sculpture could be gently attacked with the same brush, using a mixture of fine pumice powder with plaster of Paris. This should only be done in emergencies and should not be applied to a valuable piece. If the figures are not surface coloured they may be cleaned with a little butter. A wax figure should, wherever possible, be kept in a glass-case. Under no circumstances should any spirit solvent be used, as even the weakest of these will speedily dissolve the wax and the object will be ruined.

5 *Textiles*

THE MOST DEVASTATING AND THE MOST INSIDIOUS DAMAGE which textiles suffer undoubtedly comes from the action of light. Although fading is usually accepted as an occurrence which is inevitable, it should be remembered that when fading occurs, deterioration of the actual filaments in the fabric will take place at the same time and for the same reasons. It is therefore most important that every measure possible and convenient should be taken to protect textiles from strong light. It should also be taken into account that the action of light is accentuated when excessive moisture is present. The action of fading is caused by a combination of moisture, light and oxygen, and, although it is impossible to protect fabrics from these entirely, the less they are exposed, the longer will be their life and the better their condition.

Where textiles are used or stored in conditions that suffer from dampness, warmth and stagnant air, mould and bacteria growth will be promoted. Ideally, the temperature should be in the range between 60° and 70°F.; the relative humidity should not be much more or less than 65%. The lower the relative humidity and the drier the air, the greater will be the tendency for the textiles to become brittle, and this will particularly endanger fabrics that are already weak. Cleanliness of the room itself is also of paramount importance, as again dust and dirt are dangerous and destructive to all kinds of textiles. Adequate ventilation should be provided, and so arranged that local pockets of high relative humidity or stagnant air are not allowed to form.

There is always a risk of moth with textiles, but to minimize this they should be as clean as possible. Moths, like other insect pests, rely on dirt and dust in corners and crevices in which to breed, and the moth itself prefers, or is attracted to fabrics that that are dirty. Moths and other insect pests are more liable to attack materials made from animal fibres such as wool and silk than those from vegetable fibres in the linen and cotton group.

There are a large number of proprietary moth-proofing agents that can be purchased, most of them based on pentachlorphenol or paradichlorobenzene. One product particularly suitable for moth-and insect-proofing, is 'Mystox L.P.L. (R.R. Grade.)' This should be applied as a spray and as a 5% solution in white spirit. If this is being applied to the back or seat of a chair or sofa, the wooden arms and legs should be covered as the spray may remove the wax polish. This same material is also suitable for treating large tapestries. But before these are sprayed, if they are sound enough physically, they should be carefully brushed free from dust and moth-eggs, preferably out-of-doors.

A second chemical which can be applied as a spray for large areas of textiles such as a tapestry or valuable curtains is pyrethrum. This may be applied by itself or included in a safe insecticide. The spray should be from a powerful projector that will give an even mist, and the droplets should in no way damage the colour or the material of the textile.

The decision to attempt the cleaning of a tapestry, fabric or textile of any kind, must depend upon the condition of the material. If it is at all frail, or coming to pieces in any part, it is entirely a matter for the skilled craftsman and should be left to him. Some of the dry-cleaning firms have specialists in this field and they should be consulted.

If fabrics are firm and exhibit no weaknesses, they can be washed as a first step towards cleaning and renovation. In the case of coloured textiles the fastness to water of the dyes should be tested. The washing should always be in soft water, and in as large a sink or bath as possible. If it is an old galvanized tank with rough edges, protection for the textile can be given by lining the tank with a sheet of fairly thick polythene. The first washing should be in plain water only, either cold or just lukewarm. The material can be left soaking for up to half an hour, but with several changes of water. If it is found that not sufficient dirt is removed by the plain water, detergents such as 'Lissapol N' may be used. This is more suitable than soap, as it will not form a scum, and is far safer than the commercial cleansing powders and liquids, as these may contain soap powder or soda, which could damage the material. After washing with the detergent, the material should again be rinsed thoroughly several times and then, if the material is at all weak, it can be lifted from the bath on the sheet of polythene that was lining it and allowed to drain. After the draining, while still on the polythene sheet, it can be laid flat on a table and dabbed gently with dry, clean towelling. After damp-drying, it should be carefully smoothed out so that it lies in its natural position and the remainder of the drying can be completed in a warm, suitably ventilated room; it may be assisted by the use of a hair-dryer.

For fabrics with a delicate nature, or those that have to be cleaned 'in situ' as tapestry upholstery, the washing can best be carried out by using a solution of 'Saponin' which is a derivative from soapwort. This saponin should be mixed with a little warm, soft water, and applied with a soft brush. A certain amount of froth will be worked up and excess should be lifted off with swabs of cotton wool or soft towelling. After treatment, the textile should be dabbed dry with towelling, or if smooth, with cotton wool.

Stains in textiles may vary from iron-mould to ink, fruit stains, wines and even blood. This last is notoriously difficult to remove, and, in many cases is better left, as the rigorous action necessary may destroy the fabric. With the removal of any stains, risk is taken, as the solvents necessary to lift a grease spot, for example, may attack the old dyes in the material. Really, this is again a time to ask advice from a qualified person who can test the particular colours and advise or carry out the removal of the blemishes.

Candle-wax spots or grease can often be cleared by placing a piece of thick blotting paper underneath, another sheet on top, and then applying a warm iron. The warmth of the iron should cause the grease to melt and run into the warm blotting-paper. If portions of the grease or wax are left, they can be very gently loosened and removed by applying turpentine or benzene. Another expedient that may be attempted for removing recent grease spots is to lightly brush them with Fuller's Earth.

Spots of mud should be carefully loosened with a blunt scalpel and then softened first of all with soft, warm water; if still obstinate, they may be very carefully 'spotted' with a brush with extremely weak ammonia solution or hydrogen peroxide. For many stains proprietary removers may be safest, but if care is exercised other methods can be tried.

One stain that occasionally occurs in an old costume if it has been used for a theatrical production, is lipstick or grease-paint. This should first of all be tried with soft, warm water, and, if this fails, a 5% solution of acetic acid can be 'spotted' with a small brush. Ordinary writing-ink should first of all be worked at with soft, warm water, and, if this is not sufficient to free the stain, on wool or silk a 2% solution of hydrochloric acid may be tried; on cotton or linen, 'Chloramine T' as a 2% solution should be used. In each case the materials must be washed with plentiful dabbing of fresh, soft water with a pad of cotton wool on to sheets of thin towelling or blotting-paper placed underneath.

Another cleaner which is reasonably safe is carbon tetrachloride, particularly for modern fabrics, and many obstinate stains can be removed by this method. Mildew and rust stains are often very obstinate. The rust in particular is difficult to deal with as the material on which it appears will have been weakened by its presence. Gentle experiment by 'spotting' with increasing strengths of hydrogen peroxide may be successful. Whatever type of stain-eradication is tried, a very wise step is to place two or three thicknesses of clean, thick blotting-paper underneath the stain being treated. This step is suggested as the solvent when applied will carry the stain through the material and on to the blotting-paper. Further there is a risk in any stain removing of producing rings and solvent stains.

Textiles, like many antique objects, are affected savagely by sulphur dioxide (an unfortunate ingredient of city air). Sulphur dioxide will very easily form sulphurous acid, and this, in turn becomes sulphuric acid with oxidization. One of the main substances to cause this change in sulphuric acid is iron. This can often be noticed on fabrics that are stretched, using old iron tacks on canvas stretchers, the material is burnt or rotted with a dark brown stain round the head of the tack. To prevent this particular damage, copper nails or tacks should always be used when stretching any type of textile.

One of the worst features of sulphur dioxide attack on fabrics is that it weakens the fibres, and will thus cause breakages and damage that are irreparable. If possible, valuable textiles should be kept in glass-cases which will protect them from this attack to some extent. The storing of fabrics, if, indeed, they must be stored, should always be in the dark. Where old colours, and even some modern colours are concerned, it is almost a golden rule that they must be kept in the dark.

For storing materials, the greatest care before they are parcelled should be taken to make certain that they are clean and that there is no insect-infestation present. The old habit of wrapping in paper has now been displaced by the modern plastic bag. These bags have several advantages, they are non-hygroscopic and cannot harbour damp as the paper used to do, and as they are transparent the contents can be inspected without being unsealed. The pieces of fabric, dress or robes should if possible be rolled and then sealed into the polythene bag with the use of a sticky tape. Rolling prevents the weakening effect of creasing by folding. Before sealing, it is well to put a small cupful of dichlorobenzene crystals at the bottom of each bag. It is important to make sure that the textiles being stored in this way are absolutely dry before being put into the bag, because if any moisture at all is sealed in, mildew is certain to arise.

When a garment or curtain is taken out of storage, it is essential that it should be very thoroughly aired to rid it of the smell and vapour of the dichlorobenzene before being used or placed in an inhabited room. This chemical, which is a highly effective anti-moth and insect agent, has a very strong astringent smell, which can be dangerous as it is a liver poison. Inhaling, therefore, should be strictly avoided.

One of the most difficult materials to deal with is one where a metallic thread of silver or gold is present in the weave. In Plate No. 41 can be seen a Seplia Torali which belongs to the Jewish Museum. It dates from about 1750 and is silk brocade with gold fringe, possibly from Spitalfield. The trouble with cleaning an example such as this is that the cleaning materials for the brocade part must at all costs be kept away from the rest of the textile, otherwise they can cause discoloration and rotting. In this particular case, the gold thread of the fringe was only in need of washing to make it bright again; it was then brushed over with the lacquer 'Frigilene'. A more mild course with silver thread might be to use a very dilute ammonia solution, increasing the strength if the tarnish and grime does not surrender to it (Plate No. 42). Care should be taken to see that the ammonia does not reach the underlying fabric, especially if this is dyed or soiled. If the fabric is soiled, the liquid ammonia will probably leave a stain, and if dyed, it may well be severely damaged. If 'Silver Dip' is used it should not be allowed to reach the fabric as it contains hydrochloric acid which would cause rotting. If the design is intricate, it will call for very careful local treatment, using minute swabs on sharpened matchsticks to apply the liquid and to cleanse it off. The same minute swab can also be used with a mildly abrasive silver or chrome cleaner on threads of this nature.

Tapestries hanging on a wall are subjected to considerable strains from their weight alone, and if they become weakened they should be given some kind of support. One sometimes sees tapestries put on wooden stretcher frames similar to those for large oil-painting canvases. This alone, is bad practice, as it can cause local strain and damage the edge of the tapestry itself. It is better that the tapestry should be mounted on to a very strong nylon or Terylene net. Then this net can be mounted on a stretcher or the net can be hung itself from the wall, and thus take the weight and strain from the tapestry. The way in which the tapestry or textile should be secured on to a net support will vary with the type or weight of the textile in question but, broadly speaking, the textile should always be sewn on to the net support rather than glued; stitching is far more natural to the material than sticking.

Of the pieces of embroidery and sewn work that have come down to us, one of the commonest is the sampler. If not in too delicate a condition, this can be washed, provided the colours will not run. You should test them first by putting the sampler on a sheet of blotting-paper and then pressing it with a small swab of damp cotton wool. If the colour does not bleed through, it may be safe to wash it, but you should still proceed with caution. It should be washed in a large flat dish, using cold or slightly warm water with a liquid detergent of the 'Stergene' type. You should use the amount recommended for nylon stockings, and no stronger. Gently tamp the surface in the water to loosen the dirt, and then rinse in several baths of distilled, or cold previously-boiled water. If the colours bleed, the only solution

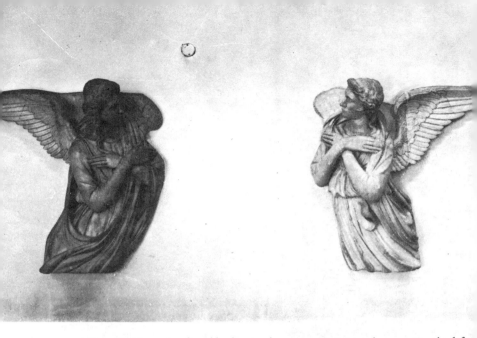

Plate 38. Example of marble cleaning by soap, ammonia and water. On the left a piece with normal smoke and city dirt. On the right after cleaning a similar piece

Plate 39. Polychrome statue in wood before cleaning.

Plate 40. The same statue in Plate 39 after the removal of grime and old varnishes.

Plate 41. A Seplia Torali from the Jewish Museum before treatment.

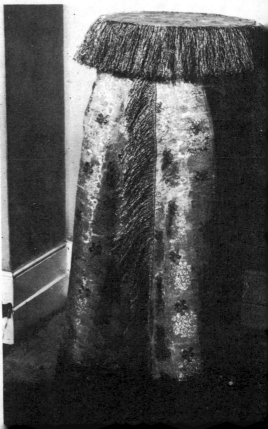

Plate 42. The Seplia Torali after cleaning.

Plate 43. The colour of the ... te muslin had become a ... grey.

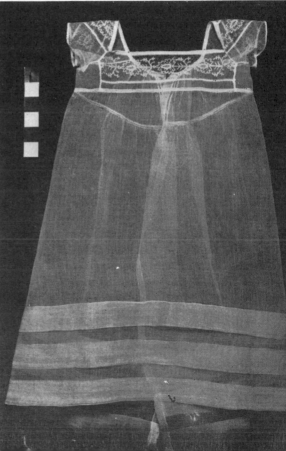

Plate 44. The muslin shown in Plate 43 after treatment.

Plate 45. *Pencil drawing of James Harding in a badly foxed state.*

Plate 46. *The picture shown in Plate* 45 *after bleaching.*

is not to wash the sampler but to have it dry-cleaned. If you have a dry-cleaner who does the work on his premises, you can persuade him to give it special attention, and many of the larger firms have specialist advice for the asking.

If you attempt to dry-clean at home, you can try this by dipping and gently tamping the sampler in a bath of turpentine substitute. This liquid is inflammable and protection against fire should be taken. A second liquid which is non-inflammable is carbon tetrachloride, and this can often be a very effective cleaner; it is, however, very toxic and the cleaning should be done in a well-ventilated room.

If the condition of the sampler is delicate, or the colours are suspect, the only possible safe course would be to dust the surface with a dry powder such as potato flour.[8] This will pick up an appreciable quantity of the dirt, and can then be brushed off. The process can be repeated two or three times.

As to mounting the sampler when it has been cleaned, one acceptable way if it is in good condition and strong, is to buy a stretched canvas a little bigger than the sampler from an Artists' Colourman. The sampler then can be sewn on to the edges round the canvas and framed like a picture. Alternatively, you could buy the stretcher itself and then choose a contrasting or complementary toned, good quality linen, stretch this on to the stretcher and then, again, sew the sampler on to this. When stretching the linen on the stretcher it is very important to make sure that you get the warps and wefts lying parallel with the sides of the stretcher. The stretching should be done with copper tacks. The first should be placed in the middle of one side, next putting the second tack in the middle of the opposite side. Now repeat the process with the other two ends, and, after that gradually work into one corner, placing the tacks about 1½" apart. When sewing the sampler into position it should be done with fine quality silk or cotton thread that matches as nearly as possible the ground-tone of the sampler, and the stitches should be as small as possible.

One of the most delicate materials to clean or repair is lace. All kinds of lace are very easy to damage. One weak or broken thread can very easily and quickly destroy the value of a piece. Lace of this nature, or lace-cuffs, should first of all be soaked in several lots of distilled water. This is to loosen the dirt. After this,

[8] See Appendix.

soak them in warm water that contains half a teaspoonful of a liquid detergent, then rinse thoroughly and pin out the pieces on to white blotting-paper in their correct shape, taking care to use non-rusting pins.

If there is a specimen of lace tacked to a pillow, which cannot be moistened for cleaning, the process should be to shake the pillow to remove surface dust, and the lace itself should be cleaned dry by using powdered French chalk and a brush to remove the chalk afterwards. French chalk and a brush are one of the safest cleaners for all types of lace.

In Plates Nos. 43 and 44 can be seen an over-dress before and after restoration. In this particular case the colour of the white muslin has become dark grey, and this disappears completely on cleaning. The material was badly discoloured with age and covered with brown stains, and between the larger ones were small pin-point stains which possibly could have been caused by previous washes in tap water containing iron.

The over-dress was first of all washed, using soft water and 'Lissapol N'. The dress was just floated gently into the water and a patting motion was used to release the dirt, no rubbing or squeezing was undertaken as any physical action such as this could severely damage a delicate fabric. Subsequent baths of washing and rinsing water were used, and finally the dress was lifted out on to a draining board. The removal of the stains was achieved by placing the garment into a bath half-filled with soft water to which was added sodium perborate at a strength of 2 ozs. to the gallon, plus a little detergent. If using sodium perborate in this manner, it is important that an enamel or plastic or porcelain lined bath is employed, as damage to fabrics can be caused if the chemical touches any exposed iron. The garment in this solution was raised nearly to boiling point, at which stage oxygen was liberated, forming a mass of small bubbles. The heat was then turned off and the liquid allowed to cool. After the cooling there was still sign of some stains, and these were finally removed with a patent rust remover containing oxalic acid. Again, the dress was once more rinsed in water, and then rolled in absorbent-paper and dried, finally being dipped in a solution of polyvinyl alcohol to restore crispness and body and also to strengthen the fibres. When nearly dry, the dress was finally ironed on the back with the thermostat set for wool.

Carpets and rugs of all textiles have the worst treatment, hammered underfoot; constantly dented with heavy castors or legs of furniture; and they are the almost inevitable resting place for all dust and dirt brought into the room or carried in on the air.

One of the most important things to do with carpets and rugs is to avoid trying to treat either the dirt or stains with proprietary materials. Some of these materials may do good, but others may produce some damage to the carpet which might quite easily prejudice an insurance claim on such matters. If they are dirty, the best thing to do with carpets and rugs is first of all to remove loose dust and dirt by using a vacuum cleaner. If the carpet or rug is slightly delicate or extremely valuable, it is safer to brush with a fine hair-bristled brush into a dust-pan, or towards the mouth of the vacuum cleaner as it is working. In this way there will be no undue tugging at the pile, and no undue disturbance of the pile of the carpet from the revolving brush belonging to the instrument.

Small rugs and mats get very dirty and can best be cleaned by washing, but, first of all, it is important to make sure that none of the colours in the rug to be treated are liable to bleed or be disturbed by water. This can best be done by trying a water and soap solution on the corner of the piece involved, letting it soak into the fibres at that point and then pressing a piece of white blotting-paper on to it and seeing if any colour is transferred to the paper. If all is satisfactory, and there is no question of it bleeding, there is no harm in laying the rug or carpet into a bath of water. It should be kept as flat and unwrinkled as possible, both for ease of getting rid of the dirt and dust that the water will dissolve and disturb, and for putting the minimum of strain on to the actual textile. Articles of any value of this nature, should, of course, be supported all the time they are in the water, and no attempt made to heave them up and down manually so that strain is put on to one part as it is lifted from the water. This supporting may be done by laying the rug on a coarse nylon or Terylene net, and this is possibly better than using a sheet of polythene, as the dirt and grime has a chance to fall from the rug and out into the water through the net.

A wooden frame with holes bored round the sides and thin rope forming a lattice can be adequate support for larger rugs or carpets, if working from a large tank. Other reasons for having a porous support such as net or a frame are that one does not want to leave the rug or carpet saturated for too long. When the articles are lifted from the water they should be allowed to dry flat. During this drying they should not be put near any artificial heat, but use can be made of something like a reversed vacuum cleaner or hair-dryer switched on to low heat. Better still, if the day is fine, they may be left in the open and mild sunshine. The best kind of detergent is 'Lissapol N' as this is gentle and will not leave behind any corrosive or other materials which could damage the carpet or rug later.

For a very large carpet, one possibility is to wash it out of doors on a fine day—best of all, a windy, fine day—on the lawn, when the carpet can be flat and on a good surface which will allow it to drain. The washing solution can be sprayed on to the carpet, and a certain amount of gentle tamping carried out with a soft bristled brush. Afterwards, several sprays of water can be run on to the carpet and the whole thing be allowed to dry in the same position without being handled at all. As a protective treatment for the carpet or rug, it can be sprayed with a liquid such as 'Mystox' similar to the suggestion for tapestry. This will ensure a lengthy period of sterilization from moth and insect attack.

Where conveniently possible, protection should be given to the pile on a carpet or rug from castors or the pointed legs of heavy furniture. Glass or plastic cups can be purchased which will distribute the weight over a larger area, and thus a hole is less likely to be forced in the material.

The only way to be certain that infestation, mildew or other damage has not taken place with curtains, carpets, hangings, cushions and upholstery, is by regular inspection. Examine both sides of curtains, lift up carpets and test the underfelts. If a colony of moths is disturbed, the piece should be taken down and removed from the room carefully, to avoid dropping eggs on to carpets or other pieces. It should be treated preferably outside or in a room without precious materials present.

6 *Books, Manuscripts,*
Water-colours, Prints

PAPER IN ONE OR OTHER OF ITS MANY USES NEEDS REGULAR inspection. Since the introduction of papermaking, a wide variety of materials have been employed in its manufacture: cheaper grades have been made from wood pulp; more expensive hand-made papers have been made from rags, and at different times unstable additives such as size have been used. As with many other materials, humidity is the greatest enemy of paper, although conditions of storage and keeping should not be too dry. The ideal relative humidity for all kinds of paper is between 50% and 65%. If the relative humidity is raised above 65%, fungi and moulds can grow quite happily on paper. If the relative humidity is lowered below 50% the paper itself will become too dry and brittle.

The effects of over-dampness in paper are often first shown by what is called 'foxing'. This may be tiny brown, orangy spots the size of pin heads when they first appear, and they can rapidly spread to be ½″ or more across and the whole surface of the paper will be attacked. This is particularly likely with some of the older papers where there is size present which has deteriorated and decomposed, causing a ready breeding ground for the spores of this fungus which is causing the foxing.

In very gross damp conditions, the fungi stains can be brown, purple, black, almost completely obscuring anything that is painted, drawn or printed on the. paper.

Foxing in books is a particularly unpleasant condition, the more so because the book may be attacked right through. On the market to-day there is an impregnated paper which can be inter-leavcd into the book. If this is done (about 1 sheet of tissue to every 7 or 8 pages) it should be sufficient for keeping the foxing at bay.

The problem of foxing is a great deal more serious when it attacks a paper on which there is a valuable water-colour or rare print. In Plate No. 45 can be seen a pencil drawing by James Harding which is in an advanced state of attack from foxing. The drawing is largely in pencil, with small areas in the background of gouache. The same kind of condition could easily be evidenced by a water-colour or print. To deal with a picture in this condition is a very tricky problem. With drawings, pastels, chalks or water-colours, the pigments have nothing like the adhesion to the sup-port that oils or tempera have, and it is extremely easy to dis-lodge them and float them off if any liquid removal of blemishes is undertaken. Unquestionably, any picture, drawing or print of value should only be touched by an expert, as damage can be done so speedily, and in many cases it will be impossible to rectify. But if it is desired to remove small patches of foxing on leaves of books, or prints of no great intrinsic value, gentle bleaching can be carried out. A mixture of equal parts of industrial methy-lated spirit and hydrogen peroxide can be made and applied direct to the spots of foxing with a small brush, watching care-fully the result as the bleaching proceeds. As soon as the spot starts to fade, blot both sides with clean blotting-paper and renew the bleaching until the desired effect is reached (Plate No. 46).

If a print has a serious overall foxing, some kind of immersion bath is the better procedure. It must be pointed out that the print should not be one of great value, and the ink should be thoroughly stable. For this method 'Chloramine T' should be used as it is a very mild bleach which will leave nothing of a corrosive nature in the paper. The material can be obtained from most chemists in the form of a fine white powder and should be mixed with distilled water to make a 2% or 3% solution. After the print has been cleaned as far as possible of dust and loose dirt it should first be submerged in cold water and then transferred into a bath containing the 'Chloramine T' solution for a few minutes. The print should then be placed on sheets of white blotting-paper and allowed to dry. The cleaning and bleaching action of this liquid will be very slow, and it may be found necessary to repeat the treatment two or three times for a satisfactory result.

Another method of cleansing a print by immersion is to use a good quality soap and distilled water. The method first of all should be to work on the back of the print, using a large, soft, water-colour mop-brush, and a high quality soap, gently working the brush and soap across the surface of the paper. After this treatment it is necessary to give a thorough washing to remove all traces of soap which, if left on, may cause a yellowing of the paper with time. To use a wetting agent such as 'Lissapol' or 'Nonex' is better than washing with soap, soaking the print in the bath with one or other of these agents for half-an-hour, and then carrying out the soap washing and rinsing. When immersing a print completely and thoroughly soaking it, it should be handled with considerable care, possibly manipulating it in and out of the bath on a sheet of glass.

Fly-marks and some mildew stains may often be removed first of all by a thorough soaking in cold water, and then, for a short space of time in a dish of hot water; again, thoroughly drying out between sheets of clean blotting-paper. It is most important that adequate supplies of clean blotting-paper are on hand, because if a stained sheet should be used it may offset or transfer on to the print it is drying.

Prints can, to a certain extent, be cleaned by dry methods. Surface dirt, pencil marks and other blemishes can be largely removed either by using what is called a gum-eraser (a large, soft, yellow rubber) or by gently rubbing with lumps of day old bread from the centre of a loaf. If you are using the bread, it should be watched, and as soon as it becomes dirty, a fresh lump should be taken. Not only the face of the print but also the back should be cleaned. After cleaning, it is a wise plan to sterilize the print as a precaution against foxing and mildew attacks in the future. One method could be to wipe over the back of the print with a solution of thymol.

Never be tempted to use an eraser on a water-colour, because practically all the colours can be lifted from the surface by the use of a rubber.

One of the most unfortunate treatments that old prints have

been given in the past is to coat them with thick yellow copal varnish. The removal of this varnish should be approached cautiously, experiments being made in the corner of the prints with dilute and gradually strengthening mixtures of methylated spirit and turpentine substitute, or methyl-alcohol diluted, or a spirit solvent may be tried which is acetone. A non-spirit solvent which can be very useful is 5% solution of ammonia in distilled water. Once again, the print should be worked on some supporting surface such as a piece of glass, and, after the operation, the solvent should be well sluiced away, either with water in the case of ammonia, or turpentine substitute with the spirit solvent. Any venture of cleaning a print must be a risk, particularly with the older print, as the artists or print-makers often manufactured their own ink from various recipes. Sometimes this ink was a very good one, sometimes a bad one, and there is always a likelihood of running up against an easily soluble printing ink when you are cleaning.

If a print has been hand-coloured with water-colours and has also been varnished, it may be possible to remove the varnish by the use of industrial methylated spirit. The print should be submerged in a dish of this liquid, the dish tilted one way and then the other to cause a wave effect. On no account should the surface of the print be rubbed with a piece of cotton wool to agitate the varnish, as if there is water-colour present it will almost certainly dislodge it.

One of the most prevalent blemishes on prints, drawings or books is wax, probably dropped when some eager connoisseur of the past was examining them. When tackling these, as much of the wax as possible should first be scraped off with a clean, sharp knife. Do this gently, a small layer at a time. Then one of two courses can be adopted: either 2 or 3 layers of blotting-paper are placed on each side of the wax spot and a warm iron is applied (in this way the wax is soaked into the blotting-paper), or the use of some dry cleaning solvent such as carbon tetrachloride*can be effective. If it is a small spot this can be 'spotted' with a brush and then liberally blotted, or if there is a bad impregnation over a large area, it can be treated in a dish. If carbon tetrachloride is not available, a pure grade of petrol can be employed. Needless to say, fire precautions should be taken with the latter and a plentiful supply of ventilation is needed for the carbon tetrachloride.

*See Glossary

Coffee and tea stains are, unfortunately, often present, and here the approach should be with a swab of cotton wool or small brush. Dampen the area round the stain with cold water and then, with a clean brush, dab on a 2% solution of potassium perborate. Then leave the stain and potassium perborate exposed to the sunlight for two or three hours to bleach out the stain. If there is still some mark left after this treatment, a second bleaching can be attempted by using hydrogen peroxide. Ink stains may often surrender to an application of 2% 'Chloramine T', and an application of 5% oxalic acid may be made if this is not completely effective after several tries, or a 10% solution of citric acid. Once again, a thorough washing is necessary after these applications.

Grease and oil stains can be removed by the use of pyridine, which should be applied either with a small brush or swab of cotton wool. With a print of some value it might be best to try to remove the stain first with benzene, and then, if this fails, use the pyridine which is a much stronger solvent.

Creases in prints or old documents can be largely eradicated by gently damping the back and then allowing them to dry pressed firmly against a sheet of glass. If the print is not an etching or aquatint and not of great value, it could be laid face down and have the back covered with damp blotting-paper. The application of a warm iron should then remove the creases and folds.

A blemish which can be found in some drawings, particularly those from the East, is darkening when there has been a white lead ground applied to the paper before the artist started to work. This white lead can easily be converted to a black sulphide from the action of sulphur fumes in the atmosphere, unfortunately very prevalent in this country. In Plate No. 47 can be seen an Indian picture of the 19th century, where this has happened. The drawing is in brush-line and stipple, strengthened from a charcoal outline which was transferred from a pounce made of gold-beater's skin. The drawing is on a native paper. In Plate No. 48 can be seen the picture cleared after treatment. This kind of defect would be cleared by treatment with a bleaching-agent such as the vapour from hydrogen peroxide, and it would need to be done in a special cabinet, and, therefore, should be left to a professional restorer. One method of fumigation which might be possible in the home is by the use of formaldehyde vapour. This is for the treatment of mildew and fungi. The prints or papers could be exposed over a dish of formalin in an airtight box for about twelve hours, although the fumes may affect dyes and colours. Another important point is that great care should be taken not to inhale the vapour.

During the 19th century and regrettably even to-day, prints, water-colours, drawings and pastels are often mounted incorrectly. You find works of this type pasted down completely on to backing-card. This is almost always done with water soluble glues and starch pastes (often of an impure nature). Therefore much of the foxing, mildew and fungus that takes place on drawings, prints and water-colours, is caused by infection from these pastes and glues, or from the cards on which they are mounted. These cards may range from a good quality example to a coarse brown straw and pulp board which, if damp, can cause staining by itself.

The removal of a water-colour, drawing or pastel that is mounted like this is an exceedingly difficult process. Any question of soaking with water is impossible, as, of course, the colour would come away. The only possible method is by physical manipulation from the back. The drawing or painting should be laid face down on a sheet of blotting-paper on a sheet of thick plate glass. Then very carefully the card should be peeled away from the back. This can be done by the use of a sharp knife, razor blade, or, if extreme care and observation are used, various grades of sand-paper can be employed. The danger moment is, of course, when you approach the original paper of the print itself. Sometimes, it may be better just to leave a little of the mount rather than go too deep and risk destruction. Before remounting, sterilization with a thymol solution or Santobrite*is advised, to kill off any fungicidal spores that may be present, and to discourage future growths.

It is a simpler matter if you want to dismount a print with a stable, oil-bound ink. To do this, lay 4 or 5 sheets of good quality blotting-paper on a sheet of thick plate glass; make these quite sodden and then lay the back of the mount directly on to this blotting-paper, and over the face of the print lay a sheet of good quality, strong tissue. This can be purchased under the name Japanese tissue, and the better varieties are made from mulberry bark. On top of the tissue lay a second sheet of glass, and on top of the glass, put a heavy weight. Leave the 'sandwich' overnight and in the morning lift off the weight and top sheet of glass and

*See Materials section

tissue and lay the print face down on to another sheet of glass. Then very carefully, using a long knife or spatula, peel the mounting off the back of the print. If it is a board mount, it will be found that it will split into separate sheets and come away quite easily. Lastly, when the back of the original print is exposed, the old glue and paste slime will have to be rinsed away. This can be done with a little water and soft brush.

To re-mount a print, it should be attached to the card frame by strips of paper which are called 'guards'. Depending upon how much area outside the plate mark there is, an alternative to this can be if the print is attached by the guards to the back-board on all four sides. If, however, there is writing on the back of the print, and it may need to be examined from time to time, the print should be carefully attached by a single guard on one side, so that it can be hinged back for examination. Where a drawing or painting has work on both sides of the paper, what is called a window mount must be used. This is literally what it says, a frame of card cut out and put on both sides of the picture so that it can be hung either way. In re-mounting a print or picture, the best paste to use is one made from good quality starch. This can be made by purchasing the pure starch from a chemist's shop, and making it into a paste with boiling water. The addition of a small quantity of formalin to this paste will assist in discouraging fungus growths.

The mending of torn paper is something that calls for considerable experience, and the best plan is to spend a few shillings buying old, worthless, damaged prints, and to experiment for oneself. Where a paper has been torn, the object is to re-lay the paper as carefully as you possibly can along its old tear. The starch paste can be used, or a very weak size, brushed on with a small brush. To the size should be added a small amount of formalin as a preservative. When framing a print or picture on paper, a sheet of Impregnated Paper should always be put in behind the mount, or the mount brushed over with a weak solution of 'Santobrite' or thymol to preserve against future fungus attacks.

It is always wise to have a cut-card mount for any framing of a print or drawing; firstly, because it vastly improves the look of the work, and secondly, and more important from the conservation angle, is that the mount serves to keep the surface of the glass away from the paper. This is particularly important with pastel and water-colour.

Drawings, water-colours and prints should never be hung so that direct sunlight can fall upon them, or, for that matter, particularly in the case of water-colours and pastels, so that strong direct light of any kind is on them. The only real safeguard for water-colours is not to expose them at all. With valuable examples, a small curtain should be in front of the pictures, that can be drawn aside when they are being viewed. An alternative to this is to put them in a hall or dimly lighted corridor, using only artificial tungsten (not fluorescent) lighting, in which the proportion of ultra violet light, and the more damaging blue end of the spectrum is deficient. To judge the amount of light that is harmful to the water-colour is not easy by the eye alone, and a light meter can be used. The internationally accepted light level for water-colours is that they are not safe when the light power is greater than 5 foot candles.

The fading of water-colours is a great tragedy because much of the delicacy and nuance of the great water-colour artists must, inevitably, have been lost. Some colours especially lakes used a century or more ago were particularly fugitive, and there is no possible way of making these colours return once they have dimmed.

The actual hanging place for a print or water-colour or drawing on a wall, should follow the same rules as for any kind of picture. They should never be hung over a source of heat, or in a direct draught. Streaks of dust-laden draught can sometimes penetrate the back of the frame if the back-board is splitting. Dust streaks can then be deposited on the surface of the print inside. One last point on framing: to-day the backing should always be one of the hardboards, and never three-ply, which, as has been mentioned earlier, is one of the woodworm's finest banquets.

Light can also affect almost any sort of paper in time. The modern newsprint, which has a high content of mechanical wood-pulp, is affected very rapidly. This can be seen by looking at newspapers which may only be a few months old, they become yellow and brittle. Unfortunately, the old hand-made papers which were used for print making will still become brown with over-exposure to light. The brown tone can only be removed by bleaching, and, as has been mentioned earlier in this chapter, this should not be attempted at home unless the print is of little value. A bleaching should not be attempted with paper containing mechanical wood-pulp. A check for this should be made, although it is unlikely to be present in a print of any age. The characteristics of mechanical wood-pulp are the presence of rough pieces that can be picked up under a strong magnifying glass. The back of the sheets may also carry a faint net-like impression from the manufacturing process. Higher quality cartridge may be water-marked.

One of the worst conditions for the storage of prints, drawings, water-colours, books, or any work on paper or vellums, is damp-ness and it can cause irreparable harm if allowed to remain. If there is any doubt, fairly regular inspection should be made and steps should be taken to remedy the defect: either move the pictures from where they are hanging, or tackle the damp condition in the room itself.

Pastel drawings are one of the loveliest, yet most delicate pictures one can have. A pastel is attractive, largely because when the artist works in this medium, his colours are as pure as they can be. With oils, the pigments are mixed with oils and varnishes which considerably alter the tones; with water-colour they are mixed with substances like gum and glycerine. But with pastel, the sticks of colour are bound together with the absolute mini-mum of vehicle, which may be casein or very weak gum. The colours rely for their adhesion to the paper support largely on the texture of the paper itself, so that the pastel picture is extremely susceptible to damage from sudden knocks. With pastels, you often see a little deposit of colours which have shaken free from the picture itself along the bottom of the card-mount, or along the bottom of the inside of the frame.

Prior to 1850 a pastel was, as a general rule, left 'unfixed'; in other words, it was without any surface treatment at all. Many artists to-day reject the idea of using fixative on pastels, maintain-ing that the tone-values would be brought down. There are two principal fixatives for pastels, charcoal, sanguine and chalk draw-ings: these are either a mixture of shellac in a volatile spirit, or the more recently introduced PVA fixative. The shellac fixative certainly does bring down the tone value very slightly, but the PVA fixative makes no visible difference at all. This is again one of those questions of conscience which constantly affect the restorer—is a treatment going to help prolong the life and will it affect the appearance visually? If a pastel is in a very loose condition and it is desired to carry on hanging it vertically on a wall, some course must obviously be taken, or the whole picture will fall away from its support; therefore, the fixing must be made. The way this should be done is to fix the drawing vertically on a board, and then apply the fixative, holding the container about 9″ away from the picture. The fixative should be applied in several layers. On no account over-soak the drawing, or the fixative before it dries will flood the colour away. Each application should dry out before the next is put on. The PVA fixative may now be obtained in an aerosol can, which does mean that you can get a very even spray and avoid any blobs of fixative which were liable when a mouth-blown spray was used.

During the past 100 years or more, some very strange methods of picture-making have been tried out by artists of different countries. These range from sand pictures, which take their origin from the work of the North American Indians, to the present vogue for collage. A sand picture is made with different coloured sands that are stuck to patches of glue or paste. If one of these starts to deteriorate, and the sand falls away, the problem is to achieve some form of re-attachment. It is unlikely that this would be feasible by impregnating from the back of the paper or card; possibly the best solution would be a surface treatment by spraying with a lacquer. This might cause a visual alteration, although this would not necessarily be so, as the grains of sand themselves reflect a quantity of light. The lacquer should be sprayed on with as fine a spray as possible, and the first application should be very light. The alteration in appearance can be judged as you proceed.

Collages are probably the most complex problem of all, because with some artists, in this type of picture-making, almost anything goes. Any type of material may be called in; cloth, hessian, velvet, sawdust, newsprint, paint layers themselves, and they may be attached to a sheet of ply or, more often, on to sheets of thick cardboard, again with a wide variety of glues which may be completely unstable. Re-attachment is possibly simpler than with a sand picture, as if it is a question of re-laying the piece of cloth or other material, it can be done by using a fresh adhesive. As far as possible the position of the piece of material must be safeguarded, and it is wisest not to peel it off altogether, but to leave one edge still stuck in position, gently peel back the other, remove as far as possible the old paste or glue, stick it down once more, and then reverse the process with the other side. Collages should certainly always be under glass, as they are susceptible to dirt and dust in the atmosphere, especially with their complex surface textures.

Lino-cuts, in black or colours, and silk-screen prints should be handled with caution in any kind of cleaning treatment, as the inks may be either oil-bound or water-bound. In the latter case, they will be very liable to run with any kind of washing treatment, and, again, will be very susceptible to damp. When examining or working on the mounting and back of any type of print, particularly etchings and aquatints, it is important that the print face should remain on a soft mat such as thick blotting-paper, rather than directly on to a sheet of hard substance such as glass or metal; as if this is done, the delicate ink lines can be damaged. An etching and aquatint are what are called intaglio prints, by that is meant that they are produced by the reverse to the usual printing process. An etching plate has the lines eaten into it by the action of the acid; the ink is forced into these lines and then the surface of the plate is wiped clean. Thus, when the paper picks up the ink lines, these lines are left standing as minute ridges on the surface of the paper and can easily be bruised, and the whole 'feel' of an etching will be lost.

The books on your shelves can easily be the homes of several types of destructive insects. The best preventative and discouragement for these insects is good housekeeping. Cleanliness, the removal of dust and dirt, deprive them of many of the places in which they would breed. If books are left in damp surroundings, they will go mouldy in a very short space of time. Do not forget that they are made up of paper, cardboard with either leather or linen bindings, also a comparatively large amount of vegetable or animal glues and pastes. The silver-fish is one of the insects that likes to live on moulds and rotting glues and pastes in a cool, damp surrounding, and this will eat the paste off buckram and leather bindings, and even some kinds of paper. If on the other hand, the books are near some source of heat that will over-dry them and, at the same time, they are in a dirty condition, there is another little insect rather like a silver-fish, but more hairy looking and whiskery, which is called the fire brat and it will attack the back of a book in the same way as the silver-fish. Book lice will also eat fungi and bindings of books, although they will not damage paper or card bindings. Lastly, woodworm will come out of its home in the wooden bookcase and chew through bindings and the books themselves. But if the shelves and books are kept clean, and mould growth is treated and removed, much of the danger from insects is nullified.

Always dust books thoroughly along the tops and edges after they have been bought in a sale, or, for that matter, a new book, before putting on the shelf. This can be done with a duster or soft brush.

One other fairly common blemish that paper is prone to is what is termed a 'water-mark'. This is nothing to do with the water-mark the paper maker puts into his sheet. The water-mark is caused by contact with moisture or an actual pool of water, and it leaves a brown streak rather like a tide mark. A similar defect is what is called an 'air-burning'. This is also a bright brown stain, and is caused where air has been able to get at the back of the print. If it is a print or sheet of paper that can be detached, this can be treated by soaking the paper in water for about twenty minutes and then putting into a dish of nearly boiling water and allowing it to cool down in this water. Most of the brown should come away, but, after this treatment the print will need re-sizing. This should be done with a good quality gelatine which may be purchased from a chemist. It is essential that it is of high quality, almost water-white. Soak a piece about 4″ square in cold water until it is soft and slippery, then pour off most of the water and add half-a-pint of boiling water which will dissolve the gelatine and provide a thin consistency jelly that can be brushed on to the back of the paper. The print treated should be allowed to dry flat on a sheet of glass afterwards.

When they are leather, the bindings of books very often become perished; this is largely a condition that arises from the material they are made of, but may also be encouraged by wide ranges of temperature and humidity changes. If the atmosphere is reduced to a very dry point, the leather can lose its substance and almost fall to pieces. One of the best recipes for dealing with old and damaged book-bindings is to use the British Museum's

Plate 47. Indian picture of the 19th century showing the action of sulphur fumes on a white lead ground.

Plate 48. The picture shown in Plate 47 after cleaning.

Plate 49. Half-cleaned portrait of the English 19th century painter George Francis Joseph.

Plate 50. Portrait shown in Plate 49 fully cleaned.

Plate 51. Oil painting on stucco ceiling with cleaned 'windows'.

Plate 52. Ceiling seen in Plate 51 shown in completely restored room.

Plate 53. Intermediate stage of restoration on an early religious painting in tempera on gesso, showing repaints removed.

Plate 54. The same picture as in Plate 53 correctly restored and retouched.

Plate 55. A transferred fresco partially cleaned.

Plate 56. The fresco in Plate 55

leather dressing which was mentioned in Chapter I on furniture. This is an extremely fine preservative for leather, and has an almost magical quality of revitalising the substance. Not only is it a preservative and an excellent polish for the covers; but, once it has dried out it revivifies the colours of the leather and will bring up the gold and metal-foil toolings used. The dressing should be applied sparingly with swabs of cotton wool; care taken that it does not get on to the pages, and the book then left to dry out standing on end with the covers slightly open for two days. It may then be polished up with another large piece of cotton wool. If it is felt that a higher degree of polish is needed as with calf bindings, an application of the cream wax polish can be made.

No attempt should be made to clean works on parchment and vellum, as the process is highly risky. The parchment, being untanned skin, cannot be treated in the same way as the bindings, the most that should be attempted is to gently brush the surface of the sheets with a soft brush or piece of cotton wool to remove dry fungus or mould spores.

Papier mâché objects, although really classed as furniture, are made of paper and paste, and if the lacquer or varnished surface is cracked or comes away, are liable to the same maladies and attack as paper. If they are infested with woodworm, the safest treatment would be fumigation, and, afterwards a treatment with 'Santobrite' and lacquer film. One point that is often overlooked is that a papier mâché tray or article should never have hot vessels put on to its surface, nor should hot liquid be spilt. If this happens, the varnish or lacquer is almost certain to deteriorate. Cleaning and polishing are best achieved by the use of the cream wax polish, which will in the first instance remove dirt and, after a period of time can then be polished.

Another and perhaps more permanent polish can be one of the proprietary synthetic wax picture polishes that can be obtained from an art store. This should be applied carefully to give an even coat. Leave for about ten minutes and then buff up with a soft cloth or pad of cotton wool.

7 Paintings

Pictures executed on canvas, linen, wooden panels, metal plates or other non-paper surfaces

PAINTINGS ARE AMONGST THE WORLD'S MOST PRECIOUS possessions. Great masters of the past and to-day have left in colour their vision and their inspiration. The legacy which they have given should be preserved, loved and respected with every possible care.

Artists in history have used a very wide variety of mediums in painting and employed a great number of different materials on which to paint their pictures. In this chapter mediums of oil-painting, egg-tempera and others of an opaque nature are dealt with, and also supports which include wooden panels, metal sheets, ivory, slate, cardboard and canvas.

It may help to understand the frailty and strengths of a picture painted on a panel or canvas if something is known about the actual process and structure of a picture. An oil-painting is a complicated layer of different materials one on another. The artist will first of all have used size on canvas, which can be linen, hemp, cotton, or even rough hessian, to make it non-absorbent: on to the layers of size will go a priming which may be white lead or a similar substance: over the priming many artists like to lay a coat of coloured thin pigment called an imprimatura, which is done to assist their first tonal inlays. When used by an artist such as Constable, the imprimatura was in some cases left showing through; his pictures can sometimes be recognized, particularly the sketches, by this heavy red ochre imprimatura left in the areas of shade. Over the layer of imprimatura will be 1, 2 or more paint layers; finally, on top of these, the protective varnish or wax and varnish.

Thus, an easel picture may have 7 or 8 layers, all of which have to be correctly applied and all of which will have to dry out, one against the other (Figures 2 and 3).

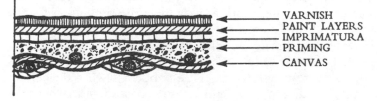

FIG. 2. Magnified section through an oil painting.

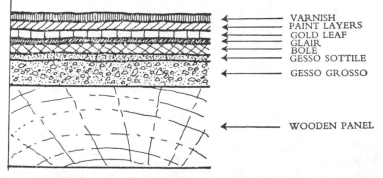

FIG. 3. Magnified section through a tempera on gesso and wood with gold leaf.

During the Renaissance gesso was very much in vogue as a priming for a picture. Gesso is, broadly speaking, a mixture of plaster with a glue. The glues or binders have varied greatly in history, from the casein curds of soured milk to Scotch glue and rabbit-skin glue; the latter is the better as it is stronger, harder and can give a very slight elasticity to the gesso layer. Looking at a painting on a gesso panel, construction can be even more complicated than with a picture on canvas. Gesso panels are invariably on wood, which may be as much as 2″ thick for very large pictures, or may be very thin indeed, down to ¼″ or less. On to this is laid the gesso, which is normally in 2 layers; gesso grosso, which is rather coarse like the hard core in a cement foundation, and on to this gesso sottile, which is put on laboriously, perhaps with 8, 10 or 12 layers, the gesso being brought down to the consistency of milk. In some cases the gesso grosso might be reinforced with a coarse canvas before being applied to the wood.

If the artist was going to paint a highly ornamented panel for a church altar-piece which involved gold leaf, both would go on top of the gesso, a red earth to provide a smooth setting for the gold-leaf and, by its colour, to give a richness behind. Over the bole was brushed glair, an adhesive made from egg-white, then the gold leaf, and finally the layers of paint which, in this type of picture, were usually tempera. True tempera is when the colours are mixed with egg-yolk, and compared with oils, where the colours are mixed with oils and varnishes, tempera is the more permanent and the least likely to damage.

One of the principal defects to be seen in oil-paintings are cracks. In an old picture these are almost inevitable because of natural shrinkage from age, but there are two causes of cracking which the artist could avoid. Many pictures, particularly of the 18th century and, regrettably, of this century are severely distorted by heavy cracking which comes about from one of two causes: first by the use of faulty materials, either impure or incorrectly treated oils; secondly, and, more likely, by the use of fugitive colours. One of the worst of these fugitive colours, which had a considerable vogue particularly in late 18th and early 19th century English painting, was asphaltum or bitumen. This colour produced a beautiful crimson-brown much sought after by painters of that period for deep shadows and glazing. Two of the greatest offenders with this pigment were Sir Joshua Reynolds, the first President of the Royal Academy, and Sir David Wilkie; they used asphaltum to such a degree that many of their pictures have become mere ghosts of what they were when they left the studios and what is even worse, they are practically impossible to clean or restore. The second cause of heavy cracking can be incorrect procedure; for instance, the artist has painted with paint layers of different composition which may be slow or quick drying: these will obviously cause an argument as they set, and they are bound to crack. More common still is where a thick, rich, oily layer is applied first, and whilst this is only skin dry a second thick layer is applied over it. Again, cracking is inevitable. The correct procedure is that the early layers should be thin. Following the dictum of the house-painter, start lean, and finish fat!

A painting, whether it is on canvas, wood, metal or any other surface, should always be treated with the greatest respect and the placing, hanging and movement should be carefully worked out before being attempted. As a picture is a complex thing of different layers and different types of material fastened one to the other, it is obviously prone to damage from two particular sources. These are humidity, and change of temperature. In the home, it is not possible or convenient to achieve the carefully controlled air conditioning and relative humidity of the modern picture gallery, but a great deal can be done to lessen possible damage to works of art by dampness and temperature.

The safest place for the picture is on a wall, but at the same time it can also be one of the most dangerous. The focal point of a room is the fireplace, and all too often it is over the fireplace that the prized work of art is hung. There cannot be a worse place to hang a picture, particularly an unglazed oil-painting. With a log or coal fire there are sources of pollution from smoke, which can carry with it various dangerous chemicals such as sulphur fumes, and not least, greasy, tarry soot that can fix itself to the paint film: more than this, with a fire that is lit every day and dies down at night, there can be extreme temperature changes, in the winter particularly, of 30° of more Fahrenheit. These can cause very considerable movement in the support or layers of the picture, which, in the worst instances can cause extra cracking, loosening of the paint film, and flaking. In addition to dirt from the smoke, and the movement from the cold and heat, a fireplace (radiators are also of course in this category) can cause convection currents which can add to temperature changes and cause movement of dust. One has only to look at some radiators to see dust streaking up the wall on top of them; therefore, wherever possible, avoid hanging any picture over any kind of heat source.

If a picture becomes dirty with age, if it is torn by accident, or otherwise damaged, its restoration is not a task for the inexperienced. The cleaning and restoring of a painting are the concern of an expert.

It is often tempting to try to remove old, dirty varnish, stains, and fly-marks, or to think that a small tear can be mended by a simple patch. Recipes that have their place in history include potato, onion, new bread and many other home-spun ideas. These may, in nine pictures out of ten, be quite safe, but in the end they will get caught out by the vagaries of methods used by artists in the past. At the best they will only remove some of the surface dirt; they cannot tackle the removal of old darkened varnish which is really what obscures the colour and detracts from the appreciation of a painting. At the worst these recipes may cause harm by leaving behind them moisture and deposits in the age-cracks that can be a future source from which fungi and other troubles may start.

Touching the surface of a painting with any kind of solvent is running a very grave risk indeed. It is a risk that should not be taken, because, if the picture has any intrinsic value, either monetarily or from a purely historical point of view, the meddling can easily cause a complete loss. To quote Sir Joshua Reynolds again not only did he use fugitive pigments, but he also employed alarming procedures in painting. One instance is known where he modelled a face in ultramarine, a procedure not uncommon, and then applied the top layers, the flesh colour, not with oils but with water-colour on top of the oil underpainting. He has also been known to put pastel and gouache on top of his oil. If instances like this are tackled by the unwary or unskilled, almost irreparable damage can be caused.

Another cause of disfigurement which it is a temptation to remove is a fly-spot. These wretched insects will all too often march across an unglazed picture, nearly always it seems across the lighter parts, leaving their trail behind them. If a fly-spot is hardened it can be difficult. If any scraping technique is employed, it can easily bring a little of the varnish film and even sometimes the paint film with it when it comes away, leaving a disfiguring light spot behind. Again, leave these disfigurements to the expert

But there are some courses which are safe to carry out on an oil or tempera that has become dirty. If the picture is thirty or forty or more years old, the paint film should be quite hard, and it can be safely wiped over by the gentle application of white spirit which is known as turpentine substitute. This will not attack the varnish film but will remove a considerable amount of dirt and dust that will have fixed itself to the picture surface. The picture may also be cleaned by the application of a wax polish similar to the fine cream polish which is discussed in the chapter on furniture. The wax paste should be applied sparingly over the surface of the painting with a swab of cotton wool. A point here is, always buy a good quality cotton wool as cheap grades may have coarse impurities in them that can damage the paint surface. As the wax is applied with a gentle circular motion, the pad should be looked at constantly to make quite certain that colour is not coming away, either as a tint or as fragments from any loose areas that had not been noticed. This procedure of examining the pad as you go applies also to turpentine substitute or any other method. If any trace of colour at all is seen the process should be stopped at once and professional advice taken. It will be found that the waxed pad will lift off quite a degree of grime. When the whole picture has been covered it should be left for about an hour, and then polished with a large handful of clean cotton wool.

It should be emphasized that when you clean a canvas, care is needed that the canvas itself shall not be damaged. Before an artist paints, he 'stretches' his canvas on to a wooden frame, and the frame itself has tongued and grooved corners into which triangular wedges are hammered to tighten the canvas after stretching. Before you start, the canvas should be laid flat on a table, and underneath the canvas in the space between the stretchers a block of wood or pile of cardboard should be placed so that it is the exact thickness of the canvas stretchers and will therefore support the canvas during the cleaning operation.

If the turpentine substitute has been used, re-varnishing may be felt necessary if the surface of the picture is very dull. If this is done, choice of varnish is best one of the synthetic varnishes that can be purchased from an artists' dealer. These synthetic varnishes have the advantage over the natural resin varnishes, that they will not yellow appreciably, and, if they have been made with a plasticizer, should not crack with time.

One of the causes of the disfigurement of pictures from the past, through a kind of overall yellowy-brown tone, was the use of the early picture varnishes which were made from such substances as copal, dammar, copaiba and mastic resins. All four of these, and others which were occasionally used, had several faults—they would darken with age, crack, and 'bloom' and thus seriously affect the appearance of the colours in the picture. What happens is that a picture is varnished, and then a strange misty effect comes on to the varnish, rather like the bloom on a grape perhaps within a few days, six months or a year. The bloom may be on the surface, or it may be underneath the varnish film. If it is the latter, the only corrective, as far as the restorer is concerned, is to remove the varnish and start again. If the bloom is on the surface of the painting, it can be removed by gentle wiping with silk rag or piece of cotton wool. If the bloom is obstinate, it can be treated with the fine cream wax polish. This will also act as a preventative if the particular picture seems prone to bloom. When applying varnish, reasons which can cause bloom include varnishing on cold damp days, the varnish itself being chilled, or by some freak moisture getting into the varnish container, or if the varnish brush itself is damp. Again, if a picture is hung in a damp atmosphere, such as a house that is near the sea, or in a climate that is over-damp, blooming may occur.

Besides heating appliances and fires other causes of temperature change, as far as hanging pictures is concerned, are proximity to doors leading on to draughty passages, being near windows and in a position so that the sun's rays can beat straight on to the picture. This last is a condition which should be avoided at all costs, as not only is there the heat change, but the direct rays of light from the sun will be harmful to the paint layer and can cause hazing in the varnish. Never should direct sunlight be allowed to beat directly on to a painting of any kind.

Other sources of danger and dirt to your picture can sometimes be unsuspected. In some houses, where central heating is carried out by a system of ducts in the walls or floors, draughts of dust laden air can play on to a picture surface rather like a hose and may, in bad examples only, affect parts of the picture. If, for example, a central heating duct comes out high up on a wall opposite to where a picture is hanging, it might conceivably project dirt so that just the top of the picture would be affected.

The hanging of pictures themselves needs care and thought. The ideal position for a picture to hang on a wall is with a very slight inclination out from the wall of about 5° (Figures 4 and 5). This fulfils two purposes; one is that the picture itself will be easier to see, and secondly, by the surface leaning out from the wall, it is not so easy for dust and dirt particles to be deposited on to it. On this question of dust being deposited on the picture surface, never allow haphazard dusting of a picture surface; for not only in some cases can physical damage be caused to the old canvas layers, but also, the duster, whether material or feather, which has probably been used previously right round the room,

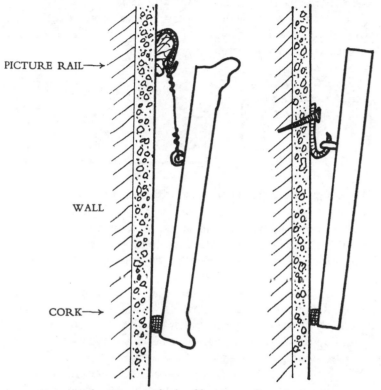

PICTURE RAIL→

WALL

CORK→

Figs. 4 and 5. Two methods of hanging a framed picture.

can carry hard abrasive fragments such as grit, and these can seriously scratch the paint surface. If dusting of a picture is carried out, it should be done with a swab of perfectly clean cotton wool with a gentle application.

The most comfortable height from the viewer's point of view is to have the centre of the picture at eye-level; this can be taken as 5′ 6″ from the floor. From the purely aesthetic point of view the frame and background should be such that they will complement the painting and not overshadow it by diffuse pattern, heavy gilding or violent contrast of colour.

Nearly every year, priceless pictures suffer from falling down the wall, the reason being that the picture wire, cord, chain, screw-eye or fixing suddenly breaks. Copper picture wire and copper chain are very susceptible to corrosion from the atmosphere, particularly if it is damp, and it is a wise and sensible precaution to inspect at least every twelve months the hanging material and the screw-eyes, clips or rings that fix the hanging material to the frame itself (Figs. 6, 7, 8).

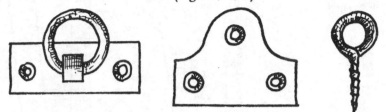

FIGS. 6, 7 and 8. Three attachments for the wire or cord to the frame.

Although a picture frame may look ornate and help to complement the picture in the surroundings where it hangs, it is really primarily a protection for the picture; therefore, it is essential that the framing should be done carefully and, most important, that it should fit correctly. How often one sees valuable pictures, either on wooden panels, metal sheets or canvas on stretchers, that have a frame which does not completely fit them. If this happens it is quite a simple matter for the picture to suffer from stresses and strains which can distort it.

The effects of heat and moisture on the different supports on which the picture is painted vary quite considerably. A wooden panel will obviously be a better insulator of heat for a paint film than a metal sheet which will instantly conduct heat changes through to the film itself. If desired, the back of the picture can be protected to help it resist change of temperature. With a wooden panel it is perhaps not necessary, but with a metal sheet or stretched canvas, a piece of hardboard placed across the back of the whole picture and fixed to the frame with adhesive tape or strips of batten can help considerably (Figure 9).

On the point of protecting the back of pictures, Christmas decorations seem to be one of the greatest offenders. Very often,

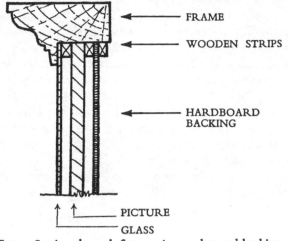

FRAME

WOODEN STRIPS

HARDBOARD
BACKING

PICTURE

GLASS

FIG. 9. Section through frame, picture glass and backing

when looking at the pride of a family collection, small bumps are noticed along the bottom of the picture itself. At first impression they may seem to be the heads of tacks or nails used in the construction of the stretcher, but generally they are foreign bodies. One of the greatest offenders are holly berries from branches hung on the frames at Christmas. Other objects can include fragments of plaster, wedges from the stretcher, and one of the most extraordinary objects was a fountain-pen which was dug up from between a canvas and a stretcher. This had apparently been dropped there by the elderly family butler when cleaning the picture rail. If this occurs, the foreign bodies can be quite easily removed with careful handling. Sometimes they may drop out by turning the picture upside down and giving it a gentle tap so that pieces of dirt and obstruction fall free. If this does not work, a soft piece of material should be laid on to a table large enough to carry the whole surface of the picture. When this has been laid face-down a flat metal palette knife can be gently insinuated between the canvas and stretcher and the foreign body eased out.

If you are taking a painting down from a wall for examination, in order to remove objects between the canvas and the stretcher or to replace the screw-eyes, hanging-eyes or picture wire, make sure that the frame and picture are laid on a table that is large enough to support them evenly. It cannot be stressed too strongly that any unnatural strain on a picture panel or a picture on canvas should be avoided at all costs. Pictures put into a frame may very often be found secured by large nails driven right through the stretcher and into the frame. This is, needless to say, an extremely bad practice, as it is often very difficult to remove these nails without damaging the stretcher and even, at times, the canvas itself or the panel. More often the nails are driven into the frame and bent over on to the back of the picture. This also is bad practice as the very action of bending over means that a jarring blow is struck on the back of the panel or stretcher which, at worst, can crack the paint or dislodge it. Pictures should be fastened into a frame by some method using a screw. If they are to be removed at fairly frequent intervals, a spring clip (Figure 10),

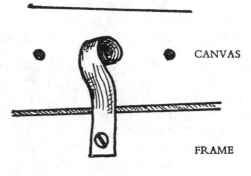

CANVAS

FRAME

FIG. 10. Spring clip for temporary fastening.

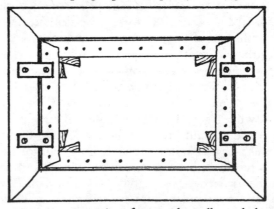

FIG. 11. Fixing picture in a frame with small metal plates.

such as that illustrated, is probably the best way, but for permanent hanging, some kind of metal plate should be screwed across in four or more places to give an even support (Figs. 11 and 12).

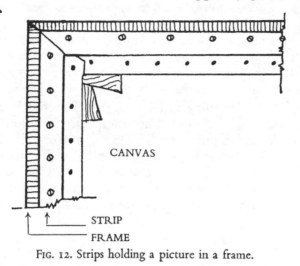

CANVAS

STRIP
FRAME

FIG. 12. Strips holding a picture in a frame.

Wrinkles may sometimes appear in the canvas, and these may be caused by the fact that the wedges driven into the corners of the stretchers have become loose or fallen away altogether, and the wrinkling can be removed by re-affixing the wedges. This should be done gently, using a small, light hammer, and making sure that there is a counterweight against the corner into which you are driving the wedges (Figure 13). One wedge should not be

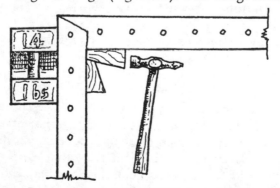

FIG. 13. Hammer wedges in against a weight.

driven right home, but you should work your way round the corners, driving them gradually farther and farther in until the correct tightness is reached. At the same time watch to see that undue stress is not applied on to the canvas so that the copper tacks or galvanized nails fixing the stretcher start to cause tears. In any case, before you start to do this, it is very wise to feel the strength of the canvas at the back of the stretcher to see if it is at all perished. If this is the case, the picture needs relining or putting on to a new canvas, and should be sent to a specialist.

If your picture is going to be sent to an exhibition in a gallery or place which will have different atmospheric conditions to your house, some kind of protection should be given to the back of the picture so as to prevent, as far as possible, different humidity reaching the picture. This can best be done by fixing a sheet of hardboard to the back of the picture. The covering may of course, be removed when the picture comes back into your own house.

Many people object to the glittering, shiny finish of a professionally varnished picture. Originally the varnish was applied to enhance and deepen the tones in a picture. It is a protective layer, because if dirt and fly-marks adhere directly to the naked paint film they are extremely difficult to remove. In fact it is sometimes impossible to eradicate them completely; therefore some kind of protective coat must be applied. Besides a varnish it is possible to give a picture a reasonably safe protective coat by a coating of wax. In the past, various wax polishes made from beeswax and other substances were applied to pictures, but to-day there are a number of satisfactory proprietary synthetic wax polishes.

If you are varnishing or waxing a picture, it is safest to choose a thoroughly dry day and one that is not too cold; the room should be as dust free as possible; the varnish should not be chilled, and it should be put on with a wide, 1″, 1½″ or even 2″ hog bristle varnish brush. The type of varnish to be chosen, as has already been mentioned, is one of the new synthetic colourless varieties. Varnishing a picture should be done as quickly as possible, the canvas or panel laid flat on a table, and the area covered not with long strokes going first one way and then the other, but rather, a series of short herring-bone pattern strokes, care being taken that the varnish is laid in an even layer and that bubbles and hairs from the brush are not left in trail. The picture should be left for at least twenty-four hours to harden out thoroughly. Waxing a picture should be done with a pad of cotton wool and a thin layer of wax put over the whole of the picture surface. This should be allowed to rest for an hour and then buffed up with another large pad of clean cotton wool.

In the past, paintings have suffered a great many indignities; they have been scrubbed and cleaned with practically every known type of liquid and sometimes with dry material. People still believe that it is safe to wash a picture with soap and water, but this is a course that should never be undertaken; first because it will have little real use from a cleaning point of view, and secondly because it is almost certain that the water will soak into the cracquelure, the fine crevices in the paint, through to the priming and the sizing; the water will semi-dissolve this size and it can loosen the paint and, in advanced cases, cause the paint to flake away altogether. On the market there are a large number of liquids and paste picture cleaners which are reasonably safe as they do not, or should not, contain any varnish solvents, so that the only action they will have is to remove surface dirt from the varnish film protecting the picture, although they should always be used with extreme caution, and first attempts should be on very small areas indeed of the picture.

Picture cleaning is really an erroneous term. What is meant is that the old varnish, which will have cracked and yellowed with time and absorbed a great deal of dirt from the atmosphere, is removed. To do this is the work of an experienced craftsman, as in most cases the solvents used to dissolve the varnish will, as often as not, dissolve or at least soften the oils and varnishes which carry the pigments in the picture itself.

If paintings are hung with picture lights on them, the matter of putting a cardboard or hardboard backing on the canvas is essential, as the wires hanging at the back of the picture from the light can very easily become kinked or twisted and it is a simple matter for them to touch and press on the back of the canvas and gradually a bulge can be formed.

If the pictures are removed from a room which is going to be decorated or for some other reason, they should be stacked in a safe cupboard or closet with a sheet of heavy cardboard between each one. This serves a dual purpose; it saves damage to the back of the canvas or panel and prevents screw-eyes or picture wire sticking into the paint surface from the frame in front of the picture. Incidentally, they should not be left too long in a dark place, especially in the case of oil-paintings, as darkness does tend to alter oil-colours.

One unseemly type of blemish which can attack paintings, particularly those in egg-tempera, gouache, and, sometimes, thinly painted oil, is mildew. This condition which is often more prevalent if the picture is on metal, marble, slate or ivory, is caused by a combination of warmth and damp, also a degree of stagnation in the air. In many houses, particularly the older ones, this condition does arise, and it is advisable if possible, to see if the picture can be re-hung, after treatment, in a more suitable position. If the mildew condition itself is in an advanced state, a professional restorer will have to be called in. But if it is in an early stage, it may be treated by gently drying and dusting off with a piece of cotton wool. As a preventative measure, a sheet of paper impregnated with Santobrite should be fixed across the back of the picture in its frame. This may be done oneself by soaking a sheet of heavy, soft cartridge in a 5% solution of Santobrite. Gloves should be worn when doing this. The material can be bought ready impregnated from Robinson's Wax Paper Company.

Fungoid attacks may also be evident on a canvas, especially if it has been relined with a glue adhesive. Relining is the term to describe putting an old canvas on to a new canvas. This is usually done with a wax adhesive made from Venice turpentine, resin and beeswax, but a hundred years ago a water soluble glue adhesive was more generally used. The fungus can make its appearance as fluffy white growths on dark patches of colour, or on the back of the canvas; this again is a condition which arises from an over-warm and damp atmosphere and the remedy is to expose the picture to plenty of dry warm air, and to rub off the fungus growths with cotton wool. Again the canvas can be backed with a sheet of Santobrite impregnated paper, and, if the picture is glazed, before the glass is replaced it should be sterilized by wiping it over with a cotton wool swab moistened with formalin.

The handling of a picture when it is out of the frame should be done with extreme care as in this state it is vulnerable, and any undue or unnatural movement can cause damage. This particularly applies to thin wooden panels which need considerable support when handling them out of a frame, and metal sheets upon which pictures have been painted. The Flemish and Dutch Schools often produced pictures on metal sheets of 20″ and 16″ and larger that buckle and bend very easily indeed as the metal is so thin. A metal sheet of this type should of course always be backed by some adequate support such as thick hardboard in the frame itself. Three-ply should never be used for any form of backing as it is the woodworm's favourite meal.

Attacks of woodworm in painted panels unfortunately occur quite frequently: as soon as this is noticed the picture infected should be isolated immediately from the rest of the collection and furniture in the room in an attempt to prevent the spread of the outbreak. If the panel is thick—$\frac{3}{4}$″ or more, it is fairly safe to treat the back with one or other of the woodworm killers such as 'Rentokil'. But if the insect holes have gone through the paint surface this is unwise, as the liquids in the woodworm killers may attack the paint films of the picture. The safest, and certainly the only satisfactory method of treating woodworm, is by fumigation with either Methyl Bromide or Ethylene Oxide. These gases require expert handling in a special fumigation cabinet and this should certainly not be attempted in the home.

In art, as mentioned earlier, artists have unfortunately brought fugitive qualities to their pictures by an unwise choice of colours and mediums; yet even some colours that are normally thought 100% permanent can, at times, exhibit fugitive qualities. One of these, which in the past was very popular with the early painters, was ultramarine. This is the real, true ultramarine prepared from the semi-precious stone lapis lazuli. In water-colour and oil, skies and areas which have a high percentage of ultramarine sometimes take on a mottled white appearance; this so-called 'ultramarine sickness' is generally brought on by the actions of acid in the atmosphere or materials that have penetrated from unwise cleaning by so-called experts in the past. Another colour that can misbehave is Prussian blue which can have been almost completely destroyed by alkalis such as ash, ammonia, soap, employed in early cleanings. These same alkalis can also affect greens, in particular copper resinate green, which is turned to brown; various lakes of crimson shade can fade and miscolour; the chrome colours, chrome yellow and orange can also darken considerably if employed mixed with flake white.

A varnished oil-painting or waxed and polished tempera hung behind glass is often very difficult to see. Yet the glass is of course there primarily to protect the painting from dirt deposits in the atmosphere. But in the average house, where the atmosphere is comparatively clean, where draught control has been looked after, and the picture is not hung over a radiator, fire or other source of heat, there is no great danger if the picture is left unglazed. If it has been varnished or waxed, there is a protective film already over the painted surface; in fact, if the house is old or in an area where the humidity is high, it might be better if the picture was not glazed, as if it is, it is yet another place where stagnant air can accumulate and mildew and fungus can find a growing place. If a picture is glazed, the glass should never be allowed to touch the surface of the painting: a small strip of thick card, balsa wood or other timber should be placed between the surface of the glass and the picture.

To-day, so many house owners indulge themselves in central heating that a new danger arises as far as works of art or articles of antiquity are concerned. Come September, the fall of the year, on goes the central heating, and almost overnight begins what can be a catastrophic effect of temperature changes. The conditions can vary considerably, depending on the type of heating, whether radiators, gas convectors, electric convectors or other sources. To obviate this damage, central heating should, wherever possible, be brought on gradually. Where you have a central thermostat this is a simple matter, and the temperature can be increased to the normal for the winter months over a week or a fortnight. Again, if central heating is used, violent change can be avoided by watching that the windows are not opened to too large an extent, and that the main door to a hall or draughty corridor is kept closed.

The collector can do much to preserve his masterpieces by control of temperature and relative humidity. Relative humidity is the proportion of moisture in the air in relation to the temperature. Ideally, for works of art, this relative humidity should be fixed somewhere between 45% and 60%. A measuring instrument will cost a few pounds, but, in relation to pictures worth thousands, or even tens of thousands of pounds, it is a small price to pay for a 'watch-dog' over them.

When removing a picture from the wall, it should be done

so as to support the picture equally and prevent any undue distortion of canvas or panel held by the frame; therefore take it from the wall with one hand at the top and one hand underneath the frame. Likewise, when carrying, give equal support to the frame, and never by gripping the stretcher. If you do this, the fingers can often protrude over the inside of the stretcher and damage the canvas.

Where there is a reasonably sized collection of pictures, a special fire extinguisher should always be near the rooms where the paintings are hung. The liquid extinguishers of varying types are nearly all dangerous for the paint film, and the better type to have is one that contains pure carbon dioxide gas. For small local fires this is particularly efficacious and will cause the absolute minimum of damage to a painting if used near or on to it.

The extent by which an old dirty varnish film can offset the appreciation of a painting can be judged in Plate No. 49, a portrait by the English 19th century painter George Francis Joseph. This is in a half-cleaned state, and on the left of the picture can be seen the full effect of several layers of resin varnish which have darkened and yellowed with age. It can be seen how the tones and tints of the picture are lowered; quite beautiful blues turn a muddy greeny-brown; pink flesh becomes a slightly orange tinted dark yellow; white turns yellowy-brown, and so forth. In Plate No. 50 this portrait can be seen completely cleaned and revarnished. In the drapery particularly, it can be seen how much detail was hidden by the thick yellow varnish and how many of the cracks (which can be seen on the left of Plate No. 49) were actually only in the varnish and have now disappeared with its removal.

An even more obscuring effect can be noted in Plate No. 51. This shows the central painting of a stucco ceiling during the early stages of restoration and cleaning when the house in Henrietta Street, London, was being reconstructed. Here the discolouration by resin varnishes is taken almost to the limit, as can be seen by the windows in the painting that have been cleaned in comparison with the rest of the panel. On a ceiling the painting takes the full brunt of smoke and fumes, as the hot air rises and is unable to escape and everything possible is deposited on to the ceiling or a picture on it. In Plate No. 52 the cleaned picture can be seen restored and in relation to the rest of the room. The picture represents 'Apollo with twins unveiling Truth and Love overcoming Hate', and is attributed to Antonia Delluci of Treviso, date 1654–1726, and is painted in oils on to the plaster.

Unfortunately, many pictures during their long lives, are subject to hazardous cleaning and over-zealous retouching and in-painting. Often quite large areas of the picture have been treated in this way, so that very little indeed of the master's brushwork remains. In Plate No. 53 can be seen a portion of an early religious painting in tempera on gesso. In this plate the picture is partially cleaned and over-paint has been removed. It can be seen in the patterning in the background behind the Virgin Mary that a large area had at some time been damaged and over-painted. This particular area would have been gold leaf, painted, and also patterned with different shaped punches. In Plate No. 54 can be seen the completely restored picture with the background brought back, approaching what it must have been when the original artist completed the picture.

Very seldom do frescoes find their way into private collections, for the simple reason that they generally remain part of the wall on which they are painted. But there have been some remarkable instances where frescoes have been transferred from the wall on to a support where they have been cleaned and are now in collections far from their native home. In Plate 55 can be seen a transferred fresco entitled 'Raising of Lazarus' by Perino del Varga. This plate shows it half way through the cleaning, and one can clearly see the amount of dirt and old varnish that can accrue on the surface of a picture, and just how much of the beauty this can obscure. In the right hand portion of the newly cleaned fresco can be seen damage caused by abrasion, wear and tear, and atmosphere. In Plate 56 is the completely cleaned fresco and the amount of retouching that has been necessary can be judged by gauging this against the cleaned half of Plate 55. This particular fresco was originally in the Mossini Chapel in St. Trinita di Monti, Rome, and dates from 1540. This kind of work is, of course, entirely the province of the experienced restorer and, with an example such as this fresco, it would be a work of many months careful and dedicated work. The surface of this fresco was extremely weak and in a friable condition with large areas of flaking, loss of pigment, the varnish film was brittle, very badly discoloured and so opaque that very little of the original composition or colour could be seen to help the restorer judge the progress of his work. The treatment consisted in the consolidation of the attachment of the pigment and ground, the removal of the varnish film and areas of over-painting, binding and attaching the colour and then in-painting and retouching with water-colour medium and egg tempera.

During the last twenty years two new types of paint have been introduced for the artist; these are acrylic and alkyd. The first is emulsion based and is somewhat similar to egg tempera, except that the acrylic resin which is the vehicle is a strong adhesive; this allows the painter to use very thick impasto, and also the paints can be applied to a variety of supports apart from canvas, which can include metal sheets, leather, heavy loose-weave textiles and various types of card. Acrylic pictures may have been varnished or not. It is important to find out when purchasing a painting exactly what the medium is. A grimed acrylic does call for specialist treatment. A picture painted with alkyd colors will appear similar to oils and should be treated in the same manner.

Glossary

ACETONE An inflammable, colourless liquid, with a strong smell. It is used as a solvent for varnish films and waxes.

ACRYLIC RESIN These are artificially prepared resins that are being introduced as vehicles for colours in painting.

ALABASTER This is divided into two types: the hard Egyptian alabaster somewhat like marble and translucent, this is a calcium carbonate; and a softer substance usually called alabaster which is a calcium sulphate. The latter is slightly soluble in water.

AMARANTH A wood sometimes used in early furniture making which is bright purple and turns a warm brown on exposure to air.

AMBER A translucent fossil resin of a warm yellow-golden colour. Used for gems and occasionally for small carvings.

AMBOYNA WOOD This was used for veneering and inlays during the second half of the 18th century.

AMETHYST A semi-precious stone with a purple or warm bluish colour A quartz coloured by manganese compounds.

AMMONIA A reagent sometimes used for removal of varnish or hard wax.

ANNEALING A term that can be used with a variety of crafts. It means gentle, slow cooling after extreme heat in manufacture. It is used to soften or relax strained metal or glass.

APRON The band of wood under a table top, which may or may not include a drawer.

AQUATINT A tint that is produced from a copper or zinc plate which has been given a speckled ground before etching.

BASALT Volcanic rock, very dark, sometimes completely black. Used since the earliest times for small sculpture. It may also mean a type of black porcelain which was introduced in 1832 by the firm of Wedgwood.

BEESWAX The wax obtained from melted honeycombs which is normally sold in two varieties: the highly purified white bleached wax and the unrefined yellow wax.

BENZENE A solvent obtained in the distillation of coal-tar or synthetically. It can be used for the removal of oil stains, resins, and for cleaning fabrics. Highly inflammable and poisonous.

BENZINE A spirit similar to gasolene or petrol but with a slightly lower flash point. It may be used as a solvent for the fresh resins used in varnishes, for wax and for cleaning fabrics.

BENZOL Derived from the German, it is another name for benzene.

BISTRE A warm yellow-brown colour produced in the 18th century for water-colour. It is fugitive and liable to fade.

BITUMEN Another name for asphaltum, a pigment used largely in the 18th century; a warm crimson-brown colour. In oil painting it is fugitive and it will attack other colours and never dries properly, causing severe wrinkling and cracking.

BLISTERS A condition that may arise with an oil painting if damp is present. This will sometimes attack the size or priming, forcing the paint away from the support. On wood panels excessive dryness can also cause this condition.

BLOOM A condition which may appear with varnish on a picture or polish on furniture. It resembles the bloom on a grape and may be caused by the varnish or polish being applied on a cold or damp day. If the bloom is on the surface, it is simple to remove; if underneath, the varnish or polish must be removed first.

BOULE, OR BUHL WORK A kind of decorative inlay using brass or tortoise-shell on furniture. Its name is derived from the craftsman who perfected this manner, André Charles Boule.

BRASS An alloy of copper and zinc, generally in the proportion of one third zinc to two thirds copper.

BRECCIA A broad collective term for marbles that are made up of sharp-angled fragments. It has been used for ornamental purposes from early Egyptian times.

BRONZE An alloy of copper and tin.

BRONZE DISEASE A disfigurement of powdery green spots or patches of pasty moist areas. Generally caused by over-humidity and exposure to chloride salts in the bronze. It should not be confused with patina.

BRONZING The colouring of plaster casts to represent bronze. This is generally done by using shellac varnish mixed with either a green powder or a dark, warm brown. Areas of highlights or edges can then be picked out with bronze or brass powders rubbed into the coloured surface and fixed with either cellulose or clear varnish.

CARBON DISULPHIDE An extremely volatile, colourless liquid with unpleasant smell and very inflammable vapour. It is a very effective woodworm destroyer but is dangerous to use and poisonous.

CARBON TETRACHLORIDE A non-inflammable clear, volatile liquid often found in fire extinguishers. It is an excellent solvent for oil and grease and for cleaning textiles of all kinds. Highly toxic. Good ventilation essential.

CARNAUBA WAX An extremely hard wax that comes from the Brazilian palm. It is found as a deposit on the leaves. It may be used as an ingredient for polishes, sometimes with varnishes, enamels and lacquers.

CASEIN A protein substance from curdled or soured milk. Used occasionally in the manufacture of gesso.

CHASING The decoration of a metal surface with a small hammer, chisels and punches.

CHINOISERIE A broad term to describe works of craftsmanship that are influenced by or connected to Oriental design.

CHLOROMINE T A mild bleach agent

CLOISONNÉ An enamelling process dating from at least the 6th century Byzantine period. The enamelled colours are separated by divisions of silver or gold.

CLOTHES-MOTH One of the smallest moths, the larvae of which are extremely destructive to all types of textiles, feathers, fur and hair.

COPAIBA BALSAM A resinous substance from certain South American trees, occasionally used as a varnish for oil paintings, and has also been found with the vehicle for this medium.

COPAL A hard resin that comes from a variety of tropical trees, used in the making of a light brown varnish. May also be used as a medium when 'run' by heating into linseed oil and then mixed with turpentine for oil-painting.

DAMASCENE A technique for decoration which involves the encrusting of one metal on to another. A triangular cut is opened with a graving tool in the ground metal and into this is hammered gold or silver wire.

DAMMAR A spirit soluble resin that comes from Malayan and Australian trees. Pale in colour, employed in making varnish.

DEATH-WATCH BEETLE A beetle similar in habit to the woodworm, although it usually attacks beams and structural timbers and has seldom been known to enter domestic furniture.

DRIERS Substances that are added to oil-colours to speed the drying.

DRY-ROT A severe fungus disease that will attack most types of timber. Its growth is promoted by stagnant and over-humid conditions. Seen as a reddish-brown fungus that spreads over the surface of the wood.

ELECTRO-PLATING An example of this is the laying of a deposit of silver onto an existing piece or onto worn Sheffield plate. The article to be plated is attached to a negative pole and a silver plate to the positive pole; both of these are lowered into a solution of silver nitrate and potassium cyanide. The passage of the electric current causes metal from the silver plate to be deposited on the article attached to the negative pole.

ELECTRUM An alloy of gold and silver. It has been employed since early Egyptian times for making jewellery and overlaying wood. The percentage of gold may vary from between 50% and 80%, the colour of the electrum likewise being paler or richer depending on the amount of gold present.

ENAMEL Glass to which metallic oxides have been added to give a variety of colours. It is then fused on to the surface of a metal.

ENGRAVING A printing method in which the plate has the lines cut into it or engraved into it by the use of a graver. The print is of the intaglio variety where the sunken lines take the ink, rather than the upstanding portions.

ETCHING A method of printing in which a copper or zinc plate is first covered with a wax and resin ground. Through this the design is drawn with a needle and the plate is then lowered into a bath of nitric acid or other corrosive fluid which eats out the etching lines. Derived from the Dutch.

FILIGREE A complicated metal-work in which decoration is applied with wires of silver and gold, employing fanciful twists and patterns. This term may be applied loosely to a similar type of decoration in other crafts.

FILLERS Inert materials or pigments which are neutral in tint themselves, but which are sometimes mixed with stronger colours. One of the most usual fillers is kaolin.

FIRE BRAT A small insect similar to a silver-fish which will eat the paste or glues of buckram bindings and certain kinds of paper if the conditions of storage are overwarm, and dirty.

FIXATIVES Solutions that are sprayed on to crayon, pastel, charcoal or chalk drawings to prevent smudging or dropping of particles of colour. They may be shellac and methylated spirits. More recent introductions are PVA solutions.

FOXING Small orange brown spots that appear as spreading blots on paper of different kinds. Generally caused by the action of damp which encourages fungus growth present in the size of the paper.

FRENCH POLISH A method of high gloss finish introduced in the 19th century. Made by applications of shellac in alcohol with sometimes additions of other resins.

FRESCO A type of wall painting in which the artist grinds his colours in water and applies them to the freshly plastered wall whilst the plaster is still damp.

GESSO A material made, in the broad sense, by mixing a white material usually either gypsum or whiting with a glue. It may be used either as a ground for paintings or as a surface treatment for plain or carved wood upon which it is desired to lay a metallic leaf such as gold. One of the best varieties is made by mixing rabbit-skin glue with fine whiting, when the resulting surface will be extremely hard although absorbent.

GILDING The art of laying gold leaf on to an object. The craft dates from very early times. To-day the term may also imply the covering of a gesso or other layer with bronze powder mixed with cellulose lacquer or size.

GOLD-BEATER'S SKIN A specially prepared animal membrane which is used to separate leaves of gold foil whilst they are being beaten to the correct thickness.

GOUACHE A method of water-colour painting in which opaque water-colours are used.

GROUND The collective term that is used to describe the coating or surface of a painting support. It may also be applied to the wood on which veneers are stuck in furniture.

HAREWOOD A sycamore that has been dyed and was used during the 18th century for inlay and veneer work.

HYDROGEN PEROXIDE A reasonably safe bleaching agent. Should be used diluted to a weak solution with water. It should be analytical reagent grade as this contains no harmful stabilisers.

JAPANNING A high-gloss finish for woodwork. It can be produced by an application of a coat of black varnish made from asphaltum, linseed oil, resin and turpentine, carried out on a gesso ground previously laid on the woodwork. It was intended as an imitation of oriental lacquer.

JEWELLER'S ROUGE A fine form of ferric oxide obtained by calcining ferrous sulphate which is employed for polishing gold and silver. Generally applied as a paste made by mixing it with water.

KINGWOOD Dark brown wood with light brown stripes from Brazil, used in expensive inlay or veneer work.

LABURNUM A light, yellow-toned wood with brown streaks, employed in inlay and veneer.

LACQUER A yellow varnish prepared by dissolving shellac in alcohol. Additional colouring material is sometimes added to enrich the effect. This may be saffron, gamboge or other yellow or warm pigments. To-day colourless lacquers are employed on metal-work, such as brass and silver, which is not employed for domestic usage. The term originally referred to Oriental lacquer, but has now been extended to other materials with similar properties.

LAPIS LAZULI A semi-precious blue stone. From it the original true ultramarine blue was prepared.

MAHOGANY One of the most popular woods for fine furniture. Mahogany veneers are generally laid on a pine base, the best examples coming from the West Indies. It has been used widely since 1720, although the earliest importations to England date from the time of Elizabeth I.

MARQUETRY A method of decorating furniture by using different coloured woods which are laid on the surface in the manner of a veneer. The term can also be applied when the work is carried out with tortoise-shell, mother of pearl, ivory, bone and metal.

MASTIC A resin obtained from *Pistacia Lentiscus* used in varnish making. Mastic varnish is one of the most common varnishes for pictures; it is a light yellow colour, but suffers from a tendency to 'bloom' in cold or damp conditions.

MEDIUM When this term is applied to the work of an artist it means the way in which he painted; charcoal, crayon, gouache, oils, pastel, tempera, water-colour are all mediums. It can also mean the liquid or 'vehicle' in which the pigments are mixed.

MEGILP A vehicle or medium for use with oil-colour. It is made by mixing mastic varnish and linseed oil with lead driers, which forms a kind of jelly. Its use is liable to bring on unstable conditions with the paint medium as it dries. It will crack and yellow badly.

MEZZOTINT A method of printing from a copper, zinc or steel plate, wherein the surface is first roughened with a special tool called a mezzotint rocker. The highlights and half-tones are then scraped into the surface and may also be burnished. The method was evolved in 1640 by Ludwig von Siegen.

MILDEW Microscopic fungi which can appear on woodwork, papers, pictures and other materials. Their presence usually denotes over-humid conditions and even when removed they may leave behind brown and yellow stains.

MINIATURES Pictures come into the category of miniatures broadly speaking when they are less than 6″ high. Miniatures have been painted on a very wide variety of materials, ranging from stiff thin card, ivory, pieces of slate, specially prepared pieces of porcelain, thin plates of such metals as copper and zinc, and also glass. They may be painted in oil, water-colour or tempera.

MOROCCO-LEATHER A high-grade leather made originally in Morocco and the Barbary States, and now made in Europe. It is prepared from goatskins.

MOSAIC A method of decorating walls, ceilings and floors with pictures built up from small fragments of glass, pottery, stone and marble set into a cement or special plaster.

MOTHER OF PEARL The lining from the shell of a variety of different fresh and salt-water shell-fish. It has a characteristic pearly iridescent appearance.

MOUNTS The collective term for card or cardboards that may be coloured or covered with materials such as textured papers and linen. These cards are used to carry a drawing, print, water-colour or pastel picture. It may be applied whether they have an aperture cut to act as a frame within a frame or whether pictures are actually mounted on to the cards themselves before being put into the frame.

NIELLO With this type of work, the design is engraved deeply on silver and then filled with a black composition, usually sulphides of lead, silver and copper. The process has been used extensively in Russia and goes back to the early Greek and Egyptian civilizations.

OBSIDIAN A volcanic glass, very hard and brittle, which can be chipped much in the same manner as flint. It was at one time used by the early people to make tools and weapons. The colour may range from black to brown and green. The charm lies in its translucence.

OGEE A term used in architecture and furniture meaning a moulding that has a double curvature.

OLIVE-WOOD A close-grained wood with light and dark stripes which is used for inlay. Comes from various places in the Mediterranean and is recognizable when new by a very pleasant smell.

ORMOLU This is a variety of brass specially prepared for castings and is normally made up of equal parts of copper, zinc and tin. It can also be prepared from equal parts of copper and zinc alone, without the tin, if a harder material is desired. Originally, it was gold or gold leaf ground and prepared for gilding brass, bronze, or other metal; such as, gilded bronze used in the decoration of furniture, etc. The gilding could be applied by firing.

OVER-PAINT To add another colour over a previously dry film. This could be applied to altering a previously painted picture many years after it had been done.

PAPIER MÂCHÉ A material for modelling made from pulped paper, usually of a cheap variety, mixed with size. This can be employed for making casts or for modelling mouldings or ornaments. The name is literally derived from the French for 'chewed paper'.

PAPYRUS A writing material used by the early Egyptians, and made from leaves of the papyrus reed.

PARCHMENT The treated skin of the goat, calf or sheep. It is prepared without tanning so that it may be used for writing or painting. Lime is used to remove the hair, and then successive stages of scraping and rubbing smooth the surface.

PARQUETRY A type of veneering or inlaying using geometric designs, generally with woods of the same colour. The effect is achieved by laying the pieces so as to get a contrast between the directions of the grains of the woods.

PASTEL Very soft crayon used by the artist in which the pigments and filler, such as China clay, are bound together with the minimum of a substance such as gum tragacanth or casein.

PATINA A term used to describe the finish on wood, metal or stone, which may be the effect of age, rubbing, polishing, weathering or other causes. Patina can have many nuances which are often so subtle that only the expert can truly judge the cause.

PETTENKOFFER PROCESS A method invented by Max von Petten-koffer, who lived from 1818 to 1901, for revivifying a varnish film on an oil-painting. It involves exposing the varnish to vapour from alcohol in a closed space. The effect was only temporary, and if mis-handled could cause damage to the paint film.

PEWTER An alloy of lead and tin. Used from early times for making drinking vessels, plates and other domestic ware.

PINCHBECK An alloy of copper and zinc; approximately 80 parts copper to 17 zinc. Used during the 18th century for making cheap jewellery. When polished bears a resemblance to gold. Named after Christopher Pinchbeck, a London watchmaker.

PLASTER OF PARIS This takes its name from the quarries at Montmartre near Paris where the gypsum is found from which it is made. Deposits are also found in numerous other places in Europe and England. It is prepared by heating the gypsum, a hydrated calcium sulphate until part of the 'water of hydration' is removed.

PLASTICINE A mixture of oil and earth which can be used as a substitute for modelling clay.

POLYCHROME A term which applied to sculpture means that it is, or was, painted. A great deal of the early European sculpture, notably the Greek sculpture, was originally painted. If just a single colour is used the term is changed to monochrome.

PORCELAIN A collective term for high quality earthenware with a translucent body, and one that carries a transparent glaze.

POUNCE A fine powder used in the preparation of parchment for illumination. Also used by draughtsmen working on tracing paper to make it ready for ink. The earlier meaning was a fine powder of charcoal, pipe-clay or sandarac which was wrapped in a muslin pad and then dusted on to a piece of paper which had a design that had been perforated with a roulette wheel. The idea was to transfer the outline of the drawing on to a wall or mural.

PUMICE A ground-up volcanic rock. May be used as a very fine abrasive or for a polish.

PUTTY POWDER A kind of tin oxide used as a fine powder for polishing.

QUARTZ Pure crystalline silicon dioxide. A collective term for semiprecious stones that include agate, amethyst, cat's-eye, onyx, rock crystal and rose quartz.

REPOUSSÉ The producing of a design in relief by working and hammering from the reverse side. A method which can only be applied to metals.

ROCOCO A kind of decoration which bases itself on shell and rock shapes. In vogue during the early and mid 18th century.

ROSEWOOD A veneering and inlay timber from a Brazilian tree, with a sweet fragrance when fresh.

SAND PICTURES A method of picture making which was first practised by the North American Indians, in particular the Navajo tribe. Later the technique was adapted in the 18th and 19th centuries to small pictures where different coloured sands were glued to a timber or firm background.

SANDARAC A spirit soluble varnish resin, now no longer used.

SATINWOOD This comes from the East Indies and has an easily recognizable light yellow colour. Popular during the 18th century and can be seen in many of the handsomely figured and elaborate veneers and inlays of that period.

SHELLAC A resin that is found as a deposit from insects on some Indian trees. Used in making varnishes and as an isolating liquid when dissolved in alcohol. This may also be used as a fixative for charcoal or pastel-work.

SILVER-FISH A tiny insect that can cause great damage to paper; in particular, bad infestation can ruin books, bindings and prints. Its other names include sugar-fish and silver-witch. It likes cold and damp, whereas the fire-brat likes hot and dry.

SNAKE-WOOD This is the heart wood of a tree that comes from the West Indies. May also be called letter-wood from the characteristic graining. Popular during the 18th century for inlay and veneer.

SODIUM HYDROXIDE Under its common name is known as caustic soda. A useful stain remover as a weak solution, but should not be employed on any porous substance which would take in the salts. Very corrosive to skin, dissolves paint rapidly. When spilt wash well.

TEMPERA In its broadest sense means a painting technique in which the pigments are mixed with an aqueous medium such as glue, egg-white, or casein. True egg-tempera painting however, is when the pigments are mixed only with pure egg-yolk.

TEMPERING The treating of hard steel to produce an edge for working on stone, wood or other materials. This is done by heating to different temperatures for the degree of hardness required.

TERMITE A sub-tropical and tropical insect of the boring variety that is very destructive to all types of timber and paper.

TERRA-COTTA This term comes from the Italian for 'baked earth' and can loosely be applied to any object made from clay that has been fired. A more practical application is to describe statuettes, figures and reliefs made from a natural clay left unglazed or painted after firing.

THYMOL A mild fungicide useful for treatment of mould on thin, frail paper or fragile textiles.

TORTOISE-SHELL As far as works of art are concerned or craftwork, it is obtained from the horny plate of the hawk's-bill turtle.

TULIP-WOOD Popular in the 18th century for inlaying and veneering. The tree comes from North America.

TURPENTINE A volatile oil which comes from the sap of the pine tree and is obtained by distillation. It is a weak solvent for varnish and waxes, and may also attack a thin paint film. Turpentine should not be stored in the light as it can thicken and darken.

VELLUM See parchment.

VENEER A thin wafer of wood, generally with ornamental grain or attractive colour or tone, that is applied to the surface of a cheaper timber with a thin glue such as rabbit-skin or Scotch.

VENICE TURPENTINE A very thick variety of turpentine that comes from the larch; so-called because it was originally shipped from Venice. It has many uses for the restorer and artist.

VERNIS MARTIN A kind of hard black varnish of great clarity and lasting properties. Takes its name from Martin, a carriage painter in 18th century France.

WATERMARKS Makers' distinguishing marks which are impressed on the paper whilst being manufactured. The earliest known examples date from the 13th century. They may consist of trade-marks, dates or initials of the factor.

WHITE SPIRIT A petroleum solvent also known as turpentine substitute. A safe diluent for powerful solvents. May also be used to dilute active solvents when they are being used for cleaning. By itself can be used to remove fresh paint and certain oil or grease stains from textiles.

WOODWORM One of the most widespread destroyers of timber. It will attack practically every type of wood. It is the grub stage of the worm's life cycle which does the damage as it eats its way through the timbers.

Appendices

CHAPTER 1.

No. 1. Before being made into furniture wood is seasoned and brought to a particular moisture content, which corresponds with a specific degree of relative humidity—which is the proportion of moisture in the air. Wood used before the end of the 19th century was seasoned by natural drying, which left it with a higher moisture content than is usual in kiln-dried timber used for furniture today. Hence if furniture made by weather-seasoned wood is surrounded by an excessively dry atmosphere such as is frequently produced by central heating, moisture will be drawn out of the wood to such an extent that severe shrinking will occur and wide members in the furniture will warp or split. Heat from open fires will not cause this damage because as they burn fresh air is drawn in and maintains a supply of moisture.

No. 2. Worm holes in the surface of the wood are the 'flight holes' from which the beetles have left. They do not necessarily have a larva in each, nor may they lead to one.

No. 3. As Bedacryl 122X can soften with heat, this treatment would not be suitable for the seats of chairs. It would be better to use White Lac Varnish instead.

No. 4. A cleaning solution for ormolu could be Alkali Rochelle salts made up as follows: 1 oz Sodium Hydroxide, 3 ozs Sodium Potassium Tartrate, 1 quart distilled water. This could be applied with a stiff Nylon brush until the black copper oxide or green carbonate is softened. The ormolu could then be rinsed under running water and gently scrubbed with a stiff brass wire brush.

No. 5. The problems of fracture and dislocation of veneered and inlaid work stem from the dimensional movement of the underlying ground or constructional wood, caused by atmospheric variations. Damage is particularly severe when the grain of the veneer is at right angles to the direction of the grain of the solid wood upon which it is laid.

CHAPTER 3.

No. 6. Glass water bottles also often show some opalescence on the inside, caused either by slight etching of the glass by dissolved acids in the water that has been allowed to stand in the bottle; or by the deposit of solids such as calcium, as the water has evaporated. These deposits can be removed, as described, with acid—hydrochloric is a useful one. A less drastic measure is to swirl vigorously water and small lead shot which help to rub away the film. Sand can be used in the same way.

CHAPTER 4.

No. 7. Many alabasters have areas or traces of original painted decoration and care must be taken that such examples are not treated with strippers or paint solvents.

CHAPTER 5.

No. 8. For cleaning samplers or delicate pieces of embroidery of a similar nature, potato flour can be used. The flour should be clean and gently warmed in a double saucepan, and it should be laid on about a quarter of an inch thick. Before cooling, it should be gently brushed off.

Formulae

FINE CREAM WAX POLISH
Pages 6 & 7

Purified White Beeswax	3 ounces
Turpentine	8 Fluid ounces
Water	8 Fluid ounces
Ammonia	A few drops

Method:—Break up the waxes into small pieces and melt, remove from heat and the turpentine and water. Stir well and add ammonia to thicken.

BEESWAX POLISH
Page 7

Beeswax	1 ounce
Turpentine	3 fluid ounces

Method:—Melt the beeswax and stir into the turpentine.

CLEANING EMULSION FOR DIRTY FURNITURE
Page 8

Linseed Oil	1 part
Vinegar	1 part
Turpentine	1 part
Methylated Spirit	¼ part

Method:—Mix together by shaking vigorously.

BRITISH MUSEUM LEATHER DRESSING
Page 11

Anhydrous Lanolin	7 ounces
Beeswax	½ ounce
Cedarwood Oil	1 fluid ounce
Hexane	11 fluid ounces

Method:—Dissolve the beeswax in the Hexane first, then add the lanolin, lastly the cedarwood oil.

EXTREME TARNISH REMOVER
Page 26

Ammonium Thiosulphate 15% solution	1 part
Lissapol. 1% solution	1 part

Method:—Gently brush the surface and rinse off as soon as tarnish is removed.

SILVER COFFEE AND TEA POT CLEANER

To remove tannin and coffee stains from inside the pots, pour in a pint of very hot water to which half an ounce of Borax has been added. Leave for an hour, then gently scrub interior with a soft bristle brush and rinse well.

CLEANER FOR ORNOLU
Appendix No. 4

Sodium Hydroxide .... 1 ounce
Sodium Potassium Tartrate .... 3 ounces
Distilled Water .... 1 quart

Method:—Mix together with a stiff nylon brush

WAX-STICKS

Beeswax .... 3 ounces
Paraffin-wax .... 1 ounce

Melt the two waxes together, remove from heat and stir in dry powder colors for the tint desired to match scratched or scraped wood surfaces.

WATER OR HEAT MARKS ON FURNITURE (A)

Linseed Oil .... 12 fluid ounces
Turpentine .... 3 fluid ounces

Take adequate fire precautions and simmer the linseed oil for 15 minutes. Cool and add the turpentine. Shake before use and soak a wad of cotton wool and apply to damage. Leave overnight and then wipe off and polish.

WATER OR HEAT MARKS ON FURNITURE (B)

Olive Oil .... 4 fluid ounces
Paraffin-Wax .... 1 ounce

Heat the two together until the wax has melted. Rub sparingly over marks. Leave for half an hour. Wipe off and polish. Repeat if necessary.

Materials for Treatment and Repair

FURNITURE POLISHES
Antiquax

Cuprinol. (Contains anti-woodworm ingredient).
Goddards Cabinet Makers Wax.
Jason's Honey Wax. Jason Antiques Ltd., 108b. Chepstow Road, London W.2.
Johnson's Wax.
Mansion Polish.
Renaissance Micro-Crystalline, Picreator Enterprises Ltd., 44 Park View Gardens, Hendon, London NW4
Rentopol Wax. (Made by Rentokil Ltd., and contains anti-woodworm ingredients.)
Ronuk.
Simoniz Homewax.
Teal's Wax.
Topp's Wax.

FURNITURE CREAMS AND LIQUID POLISHERS
Furmoto.
Johnson's Liquid Wax.
Lavapine.
Maple.
Min.
Nova.
O'Cedar.
Pride.
Rentopol. (Contains anti-woodworm ingredient.)
Spix. (Made by Ronuk.)
1001.
Topps.

GENERAL CLEANER DEEP-SET DETAILS
Groom Stick. Picreator Enterprises (see above)
In Aerosol containers:—
    Lustretone.
    O'Cedar.
    Pledge. (Johnson's.)

Slave.
Tone. (Simoniz.)

METAL POLISHES

Bluebell. (Brass, Copper, Pewter, Zinc.)
Brasso. (Bass and copper.)
Duraglit. (Silver.)
Duraglit. (Brass, copper, pewter.)
Furmoto. (Silver.)
Goddard's Glow. (Pewter and steel.)
Goddard's Long Term. (Silver.) Not only cleans and polishes but leaves a barrier against tarnish.
Goddard's Silver Dip. (Electro–chemical tarnish remover.)
Godard's Silver Foam.
Goddard's Silver polish.
Mepo. (Brass, copper, pewter and zinc.)
Meritas. (Brass, copper, pewter, steel, tin, zinc.)
Shinio. (Brass, copper, pewter, steel.)
Silvo. (Silver, electro–plate, pewter, chromium.)
Town Talk. (Silver.)
Town Talk Silver Foam

LACQUER

Ercaline. (Copper, brass, bronze, pewter etc.) W. Canning & Co., Birmingham, 18.
Frigilene. (Silver, copper, brass, bronze, pewter etc.) W. Canning & Co., Birmingham, 18.
Silver Shield. (A long term protective coat that has to be applied at the works.) Monarch Shield Co., Ltd., Hatton Garden, London.

WOODWORM DESTRUCTION

Cuprinol.
British Wood Preserving Association, Evelyn House, 62, Oxford Street London W1
Rentokil.
Shelltox.

TIMBER PRESERVATION

Cuprinol. Wood Preservative.
Rentokil. Dry Rot fluid.
Rentokil Wood Preservative.
Topane Wood Preservative.

LEATHER

Leather Dressing Solution. Hopkin & Williams. Chadwell Heath Essex, England

Renaissance Leather Reviver. Ricreation Enterprises Ltd. (see above)

Connolly's Cee Bee Hide Food

Pliancreme. (Dressing.) Arthur Rich & Partners Ltd., Factory A.2, Treforest Trading Estate, Pontypridd, Glam.

Pliantine. (Preserver and dressing.) Arthur Rich & Partners Ltd., Factory A.2, Treforest Trading Estate, Pontypridd, Glam.

Pliancote. (Lacquer coating for leather and textile book coverings.) Arthur Rich & Partners Ltd., Factory A.2, Treforest Trading Estate, Pontypridd, Glam.

IMPREGNATED PAPER

Robinson Waxed Paper Co., Ltd., Fishponds, Bristol.

SPOT AND STAIN REMOVERS

B.30 Soap. Howards of Ilford Ltd., Essex.
Beaucaire. (Oil, grease, tar.)
Coliclean.
Dabitoff. (Oil, grease, tar.)
Jenolite. (Bath stain remover.)
Movol. (Iron mould remover.)
Solvex.
Spraycleen.
Teal's Dri-Cleen.
Thawpit.

MOTH PROOFING

Drummer Moth Proofer.
Hero.
Rentokil Moth Proofer.
Secto.
Shelltox.

MOULD PROOFING

Mystox L.P.L. (Rot, moth.)
Santobrite.
Mystox L.P. 2. (particularly for leather.)

RUST REMOVERS

Ataka.
Capalla.
Jenolite Jelly.

Jenolite Liquid.
Plus-Gas.
Rustex.

PAINT STRIPPERS
Joy Paint Stripper. (Jelly).
Nitromors.
Polystrippa.

DETERGENTS
Lissapol – N.
Teepol. (Carpets, furnishings, leather).

COATING FOR RUSHWORK, CANE AND BASKETWORK
Bedacryl 122X

Araldite, CY.219. and 103.
Borden.
Bostik Bond P.V.A.
Bostik 1, Clear.
Bostik 3.
Bostik 528.
Cascomite. 'One shot'.
Casco Contact Clear.
Casco Glue-All.
Casco P.V.A.
Casco Resin.
Copydex.
Croid Polystik.
Durofix.
Evostick (impact).
Holdtite.
LePage Suregrip.
Locktite.
Polybond.
Q.5. (aerosol).
Sintolite (stone).
Titebond.
Tritone. 125 (stone).
Tug (wood).
UHU
Unibond
White Cement

SCRATCH REMOVER
Markof.

WASHING FRAGILE TEXTILES
Saponin (Saponania, Culpepper).

TEXTILE CLEANING PRODUCTS
1001 Dri-Foam.
Bissell De Luxe Upholstery Kit.

U.S.A. Materials for Treatment and Repair

FURNITURE POLISHES

Johnson's

Kahn's Prepared Wax.

Renaissance Micro-Crystalline. Talas. 130 Fifth Avenue New York 10022

FURNITURE CREAMS AND LIQUID POLISHES

Johnson's.

Minwax.

GENERAL CLEANER DEEP-SET DETAILS

Groom/Stick. Talas (see above)

METAL POLISHES

Goddard's Non-Mercurial Plate Powder.

Griffin Microsheen (Iron and Tin.)

Hagerty's Silver Foam.

International Silver Cleaner.

Krylon.

Never Dull Magic Wadding.

Noxon (Brass, Copper, Pewter.)

Silverbath.

Stieff Pewter Cleaner.

Tarnishield (Silver).

3M Brass.

LACQUER

Feroxolene.

Krylon.

Sil-Spray.

Van-Oil.

WOODWORM DESTRUCTION

Decays-Not.

Pentide.

Wood Life.

Xylamon.

LEATHER

Lexol.

Renaissance Leather Reviver, Talas. (See above)

MOTH PROOFING

Black Flag.
Tinolan.

RUST REMOVERS

Chemtron-C.
Nox-Rust.

PAINTER STRIPPERS

Bulldog Brand.
Dullfix.
TM-4.
Zipp-Off.

DETERGENTS

Igepal CA Extra.
P.N. 700.
Vee.

ADHESIVES

Cat's Paw Rubber Cement.
Duco Cement (especially unglazed pottery).
Duro E-Pox-E.
Elmer's Glue-All.
Elmer's Polymer Emulsion.
Franklin's Polymer Emulsion.
Hysol Epoxy-Patch Kit 1C.
Le Page Bondfast.
Plastic Resin Glue.
Plastic Steel (Metals).
Weldwood Contact Cement.
Weldwood Plastic Resin.

Index